D & S Vol. 20

MORE DERATIVES PART 3

B-17 FLYING FORTRESS

 in detail & scale

Alwyn T. Lloyd

AERO
A division of TAB BOOKS Inc.
Blue Ridge Summit, PA 17214

Copyright © 1986 BY DETAIL & SCALE, INC.

All rights reserved. No part of this publication may be reproduced in any form, stored in a retrieval system, or transmitted by any means, electronic, mechanical, or otherwise, except i a review, without the written consent of Detail & Scale, Inc.

This book is a product of Detail & Scale, Inc., which has sole responsibility for its content and layout. Published and distributed in the United States by TAB BOOKS Inc. and in London and Melbourne by Arms and Armour Press.

CONTRIBUTORS

Dana Bell	Hanna Massie
Steve Birdsall	David W. Menard
Cliff Bossie	Norman Pealing
Peter M. Bowers	Marilyn A. Phipps
Walter J. Boyne	Capt. John Poole
Herbert J. Coleman	Matthew Rodina
Robert Ferguson	Victor D. Seely
John F. Fuller	Don Spering
Harry S. Gann	Warren Thompson
Edward M. Grabowski	Al Trendle
William Greenhalgh	Joe Vollemeck
Gerrard Hasselwander	Hal T. Ward
Lloyd S. Jones	Jack Wecker
Bert Kinzey	Vivian White
Phillip G. Mack	Gordon S. Williams

Air Force Logistics Command Office of History, Wright-Patterson AFB
Air Weather Service Historian, Scott AFB
Alfred F. Simpson Historical Research Center, Maxwell AFB
Defense Audiovisual Agency
McDonnell Douglas Company
Lockheed Aircraft Company
National Air and Space Museum
USAF Museum, Wright-Patterson AFB

FIRST EDITION
FIRST PRINTING

Published in United States by

TAB BOOKS Inc.
P.O. Box 40
Blue Ridge Summit, PA 17214

Library of Congress Cataloging
in Publication Data
(Revised for Vol. 3)

Lloyd, Alwyn T.
  B-17, flying fortress.
    (Detail & Scale series)
    Pt. 3 published by TAB Books, Blue Ridge Summit, PA.
    Pt. 2 issued as v. 11 of series; pt 3 issued as v. 20 of series.
    Bibliography: pt. 1, p. 72.
    Contents: pt. 1. Production versions—pt. 2. Derivatives—pt. 3. [without special title]
    1. B-17 bomber. I. Moore, Terry D. II. Title.
UG1242.B6L56 1981 623.74'63 81-67592
ISBN 0-8168-5029-1 (pbk.)

Published in Great Britain in 1986
by Arms and Armour Press
2-6 Hampstead High Street
London NW3 1QQ

Distributed in Australia by
Capricorn Link (Australia) Pty. Ltd.,
P.O. Box 665,
Lane Cove, New South Wales
2066, Australia

British Library Cataloging in
Publication Data

Alwyn T. Lloyd
  B - 17 Flying Fortress.
  Pt. 3
  1. B - 17 bomber
  I. Title
  623.74'63 UG1242.B6
ISBN 0-85368-655-6

Front Cover: Drone TB-17G-85-DL, s/n 44-83519, undergoing checkout at Stickell Field, Eniwetok Island.
(USAF K15860)

Rear Cover: B-17G-95-VE, s/n 44-85507, served as N5116N, depicted here in the personal markings of Col. Robert J. McCormick, Publisher of the Chicago Tribune.
(G.S. Williams)

INTRODUCTION

Right side view of TWA's Model 299AB. (Boeing 97288B)

In the B-17 (Part 3) in Detail & Scale, (D&S Volume 20), Al Lloyd completes his three-part coverage of the Flying Fortress. Part 1 (D&S Volume 2) began with the prototypes and covered all production versions through the B-17G. Part 2 (D&S Volume 11) covered many of the derivatives of the B-17. These included the SB rescue versions, PB-1G, PB-1W, XB-38, fifth engine test aircraft, and others.

Part 3 covers the remaining important derivatives of America's most famous bomber of World War II. First is the XB/YB-40 bomber escort aircraft. This was an attempt to load down the B-17 with defensive armament in order to provide protection against German air attacks. Although a number of YB-40s were built, the program was not a true success. Included is a five-view drawing of the XB-40, and detailed information on the use of the aircraft in combat.

Stand-off weapons are shown next, and these include standard bombs with wings that were among the first glide bombs, and the JB-2, the American V-1 Buzz Bomb.

One of the most interesting projects was the use of "war weary" B-17s as flying bombs under the program names of Aphrodite and Castor. Although the results of these experiments proved insignificant, they still were important examples of attempts by the USAAF to develop flying guided bombs to hit important and highly defended targets. In project Batty, radio controlled glide bombs were carried by B-17s in another attempt at remote controlled operations. This may well have been one of the first uses of "smart bombs" that make up an important part of today's aerial arsenal.

Other derivatives covered in this volume include the photo recon versions of the B-17s, the B-17 drones and drone controllers. Project Reed, an attempt to add more defensive firepower to the B-17, the ETB-17 Electronics Aircraft, and the wingtip gunner's station experiment are also shown. Weather recon B-17s, the All Weather Flying Center, and Cloud Physics Aircraft were all weather related uses of the Flying Fortress in World War II and afterwards. Operation Crossroads involved the use of flying B-17 drones through atomic clouds in post-war nuclear testing. With drawings and detailed photographs, these important aircraft in the early development of nuclear weapons are covered in details never before published. Rounding out the derivatives included in this part are civilian modifications. B-17 spray aircraft, the Model 299AB, and B-17s restored to represent warbirds are all covered.

Throughout this volume are many photographs of these unusual and important B-17 derivatives that have been retrieved from Boeing, USAF, and private collections. Most of these photos have never been published before. The result of author Lloyd's research is a rare and informative look at these often-forgotten variants of the B-17 that are usually not included in most publications about the Flying Fortress.

A short modeler's section is included to explain converting existing B-17 kits into some of the derivatives covered in this volume. Additionally, every effort has been made throughout to point out and show detailed photographs and drawings of all changes, particularly those that are external, for each derivative. These include antennas, spoilers, scoops, fairings, windows, and any other item that would have to be added to or deleted from a model kit in order to build the derivative involved. This was done to provide a reference for modelers who may want to convert existing B-17 kits into some of these interesting and often colorful variants.

XB/YB-40 BOMBER ESCORT

The prototype XB-40, 41-24341, on the Lockheed-Vega flight line on November 14, 1942. This aircraft was the second B-17F-1-BO, which was delivered to Vega as a manufacturing trainer when Vega began building B-17s. As pictured here, the aircraft has the original un-staggered waist, a Martin turret in the radio compartment hatch, and a chin turret.

(Lockheed B-2196)

Early bomber operations in the European theater revealed the vulnerability of the bomber formations to frontal fighter attacks. The then conventional escort fighters did not have the range to escort the bombers, and, as a consequence, the bombers had to go it alone much of the way. The inability of the bombers to effectively repel enemy fighter attacks forced the curtailment of daylight bombing in favor of the less effective night missions. Attrition rates experienced by the VIII Bomber Command in the early days of daylight bombing would have resulted in approximately a 400% loss in the first year of operations. Experience gained by the Royal Air Force was passed on to the United States Army Air Corps prior to the American entry into the war. These British reports resulted in an armed escort bomber project which was begun on June 25, 1941.

The Technical Staff, Experimental Engineering Section, Materiel Division, at Wright Field, requested the Design Unit of the Aircraft Laboratory to initiate design studies for a "convoy-protector" type aircraft. High priority was placed on these studies by the Technical Staff. These studies resulted in a conference on April 1, 1942. This conference was held in the Office of the Director of Military Requirements in Washington, D.C. On April 9, 1942, the Directorate of Military Requirements issued a letter to proceed with development of a bombardment escort plane.

Negotiations concluded on May 19, 1942, resulted in Vega Aircraft being assigned the task of converting a B-17F into an escort aircraft. This aircraft would have increased fire power through additional guns and turrets, increased armor plate, and would have carried a maximum amount of ammunition. Originally, plans called for having this aircraft powered by Allison V-1710 engines. However, this action was already being taken through the XB-38 program. Concurrent with the Vega modification program, Boeing was directed to investigate the military characteristics for future development of an escort airplane. Because the Experimental Engineering Section at Wright Field was primarily interested in the quick conversion of an existing bombardment aircraft, request for further action by Boeing was rescinded on June 2, 1942.

On July 2, 1942, the Experimental Engineering Section informed the Army Air Force Plant Representative (AAFPR) at Vega that a B-17F was being modified to incorporate a Bendix chin turret. These changes were being made at Cheyenne, Wyoming, Modification Center. Previously, a new tail gun made by United Shoe Manufacturing Corporation (USMC) had been installed. This aircraft was to be ferried to Eglin Field, Florida, for testing, and Vega was invited to send personnel to observe the installation while the aircraft was still in Cheyenne.

Vega Aircraft was requested to submit a proposal on an escort conversion on July 11, 1942. Specifically, this conversion was to include the following items: (1) USMC waist guns, (2) a Martin turret in the radio compartment, (3) revised armor, (4) ammunition provisions, and (5) a fairing over the Bendix chin turret. The conversion was to be scheduled on an expedited basis using experimental techniques, both in construction and data presentation. An extra set of sample parts was to be provided in order to expedite future construction of the requisite parts in quantity. The Cheyenne-modified B-17F was scheduled to arrive at the Vega plant on September 10. Scheduling of the Bendix chin turret affected the turret installation and subsequent tests at Eglin Field.

A supplemental Request for Proposal was submitted to

1. BENDIX LOWER RETRACTABLE CHIN TURRET ... 400 ROUNDS PER GUN
2. SPERRY MODEL BT-44-UD-104 UPPER FORWARD TURRET ... 400 ROUNDS PER GUN
3. MARTIN MODEL 250CE4 UPPER REAR TURRET ... 400 ROUNDS PER GUN
4. BRIGGS LOWER SEMI-RETRACTABLE TURRET ... 600 ROUNDS PER GUN
5. USMC POWER BOOSTED TWIN 50 CALIBRE SIDE GUNS ... 300 ROUNDS PER GUN
6. USMC POWER BOOSTED TWIN 50 CALIBRE TAIL GUNS ... 550 ROUNDS PER GUN
7. RESERVE AMMUNITION FOR CHIN TURRET ... 400 ROUNDS PER GUN
8. RESERVE AMMUNITION FOR UPPER FWD. TURRET ... 400 ROUNDS PER GUN
9. RESERVE AMMUNITION FOR ALL STATIONS ... FOUR 200 ROUND BOXES AND TWENTY 150 ROUND BOXES
10. AMMUNITION BOXES FOR TAIL GUNS ... 300 ROUNDS PER GUN
    250 ROUNDS PER GUN IN TRACKS
11. USMC HYDRAULIC SYSTEM FOR SIDE GUNS
12. USMC HYDRAULIC SYSTEM FOR TAIL GUNS
13. ARMOR PLATE FOR CREW PROTECTION
14. ARMOR PLATE FOR POWER PLANT PROTECTION

The armor and armament changes for the XB-40 are shown in this drawing. (Lockheed B2874)

Vega on July 27, 1942. The Vega proposal was to be based on delivery of the aircraft from Cheyenne by August 1. Modifications were to include installation of the Bendix chin turret in lieu of the mock-up presently installed, and complete installation of a Briggs semi-retractable lower turret. This conversion was to be completed by August 20. Then the aircraft was to be ferried to Eglin Field in order to test the Bendix chin turret. After testing, the aircraft would be returned to Vega for completion of the modifications. On August 5, 1942, Vega submitted a proposal with a total estimated cost of $102,882, plus a fixed fee of $6,173, making a total of $109,055. In order to meet the tight schedule, Vega had already begun work on the project and requested that the contract be issued as soon as possible. Certain gambles had to be taken in order to make short flow programs succeed.

The second B-17F-1-BO, serial number 41-24341, was destined to be the sole XB-40. This aircraft was delivered to Vega on August 2, 1942, and contained the mock-up Bendix chin turret and a USMC power-operated tail gun installation. The Briggs ball turret arrived at Vega on the following day. The Martin upper turret came in on August 6.

Production of the B-40s was allocated to Douglas-Tulsa. Here a line-up of Vega-built B-17Fs undergo modification into YB-40s. (Douglas T81147)

Left rear quarter view of the XB-40. (USAF 29155AC)

Installation of the Martin turret in the radio compartment commenced on August 7. August 10th was the date scheduled for installation of the Briggs ball turret. The USMC waist guns were scheduled for shipment from their manufacturer in Boston on August 19th. Testing at Eglin Field was now scheduled for September 5, 1942.

In actuality, the XB-40 arrived at Eglin on November 19, 1942. The entire test program was conducted by the Army Air Forces Proving Ground Command in six days. According to the test reports, several minor changes were suggested for the armament systems. The most major suggestion regarding the armament installation was for moving the right waist position 40 inches forward in order to afford the gunners unhampered operation. This requirement for staggering the waist positions was believed to be so important that it was recommended for all of the future YB-40s, even though it would delay delivery to the field. Tactical suitability tests run on the XB-40 concluded that, in general, the XB-40 had the same flight characteristics as the B-17F. The rate of climb and speed for the XB-40 was slightly below those on the B-17F, but maneuverability was considered to be similar. Minor changes in the armor were suggested. The tests also concluded that the XB-40 was suitable for use as a bomber escort.

On October 7, 1942, a program for obtaining six modified B-17s by April 1943 was put into effect. The requirement was increased to thirteen aircraft on October 11th. Engineering for the YB-40 program was to be conducted by Vega Aircraft, while the actual conversion was to be accomplished by Douglas Aircraft at their Tulsa Modification facility.

While the U.S. involvement in the Pacific War was immediate upon the attacks on Pearl Harbor and bases in the Philippines, establishment of the Army Air Forces in England took months. Planning, organizing, training, and materiel build-up, along with a defining of effort between the U.S. and Allied Forces, took time. The first B-17 arrived in the British Isles on July 1, 1942. By July 27, the first bomb group was complete with both air and ground echelons -- this was the 97th BG. On August 17, 1942, the VIII Bomber Command launched its first attack using twelve B-17s from the 97th BG escorted by RAF Spitfires. Three more missions were flown before the next B-17 unit, the 92nd BG, arrived in England. By early October, thirteen missions had been flown with only two losses. On November 23, the Luftwaffe fighter tactics changed from rear to frontal attacks, and the picture for daylight strategic bombing changed by the end of 1942. In four and one-half months of operation, ninety-nine heavy bombers (both B-17s and B-24s) were lost, and over 100 suffered damage due to enemy action. While a 10% attrition rate was deemed the maximum acceptable, this figure actually rose to 20%. As a result, the VIII Bomber Command requested that high priority be given to improving the frontal fire power on the bombers and the development of the bomber escort. Existing .30 caliber guns in the aircraft noses were replaced by .50 caliber guns. Additional .50 caliber guns were added in cheek installations. These modifications were carried out at bases in England and at modification centers in the United States.

On January 2, 1943, Douglas Aircraft submitted a proposal for the conversion of the initial thirteen YB-40s. This

Table 1

	YB-40	B-17F
Estimated gross weight:	58,000 lbs*	54,280 lbs
(a) Fuel	1,700 gal (US)	2,500 gal (US)
(b) Ammunition (.50 cal.)	10,700 rounds	1,600 rounds
(c) Bombs	None	None
(d) Crew	9 men	10 men
(e) Gunners' Windows	Open	Open
(f) Armor Plate	As Installed	As Installed

* Based on an empty weight of 40,666 pounds (which was given verbally by the Wright Field project officer). It was believed that the airplane actually weighed over 60,000 pounds in this test.

proposal estimate came to a total of $469,820.00. Contract W535 AC-32123 was entered into with Douglas. This was a cost-plus-a-fixed-fee contract in the amount of $405,600.00.

On January 22, 1943, a requirement for an eleventh crew member was made on the YB-40. This position was known as an ammunition stocker. The airplanes were to be modified to include the required oxygen bottles and mask, and associated interphone equipment.

The 9th Bombardment Group (heavy), Orlando Air Base, conducted tests to determine the tactical suitability of the YB-40 when used in conjunction with B-17Fs. These tests were conducted in early April 1943. A pair of B-17Fs and three YB-40s were used in the testing. The tests were conducted under the condition shown in Table 1.

Ammunition aft of station six was moved into the radio compartment before takeoff and before landing. During flight all crew members were in position and the ammunition was distributed as follows:

Location	Rounds
Nose	2200
Front Top Turret	2500
Aft Top Turret	3300
Ball Turret	300
Waist Guns	1200
Tail Guns	1200
Total:	10,700

During the tests, cowl flaps were in the "trail" position for climb, mixture was "rich", and the air cleaner was closed.

Two B-17Fs led a formation of three YB-40s to a true altitude of 24,600 feet (temperature -20°C), where the formation flew level for twenty minutes. All guns were fired at this altitude and functioned satisfactorily.

The test concluded that the YB-40 would be suitable for an escort aircraft for the B-17F. For safety, it was recommended that runway lengths of 7,000 feet be used. The YB-40 should be used as the lead aircraft in a B-17 formation until just prior to the bomb run when the YB-40 would trade positions with a regular B-17. Because of concern over icing, it was recommended that the chin gun zippers be replaced with metal slides. Installation of new heavier duty B-17 brakes was suggested. No adverse center of gravity (CG) conditions were noticed during these tests.

Major Robert B. Keck had been instrumental in developing a number of the armament changes on the B-17s assigned to the 92nd BG. He was sent back to the United States in January 1943 to help in the development of the YB-40. A group of thirteen flight crews joined up with their aircraft at Biggs Field in March 1943. After a check out and a few practice missions, the crews flew their YB-40s to Montbrook Field, Florida. During the month of April the crews racked up almost forty hours of training in their aircraft. Special Orders 118, dated April 28, 1943, from the AAF School of Applied Tactics, called for the dispatch of the thirteen YB-40s. Under the command of Major Keck, the unit flew from Montbrook to Mitchell Field, New York; Presque Isle, Maine; Goose Bay, Labrador; Neeks Field, Scotland; Prestwick, Scotland; Grafton-Underwood, and then Alconbury, England. One of the aircraft ran low on fuel and landed in a peat bog near Stornaway, Scotland. This aircraft carried serial number 42-5735. The remaining twelve YB-40s became operational with the 327th BS, 92nd BG, at Alconbury.

The first combat mission flown by the YB-40s was on May 29, 1943. The target, St. Nazaire, provided a 1,000 statute-mile mission. One aircraft flew as right wing man on the 305th BG lead aircraft. A second YB-40 flew the same position on the 92nd BG lead aircraft. The remaining six YB-40s flew as the low squadron for the 92nd BG, and, as such, were low squadron of the lead combat wing. Aircraft S/N 42-5741 aborted due to loss of its No. 2 supercharger. A summary of the YB-40 performance on this mission is shown in Table 2.

YB-40

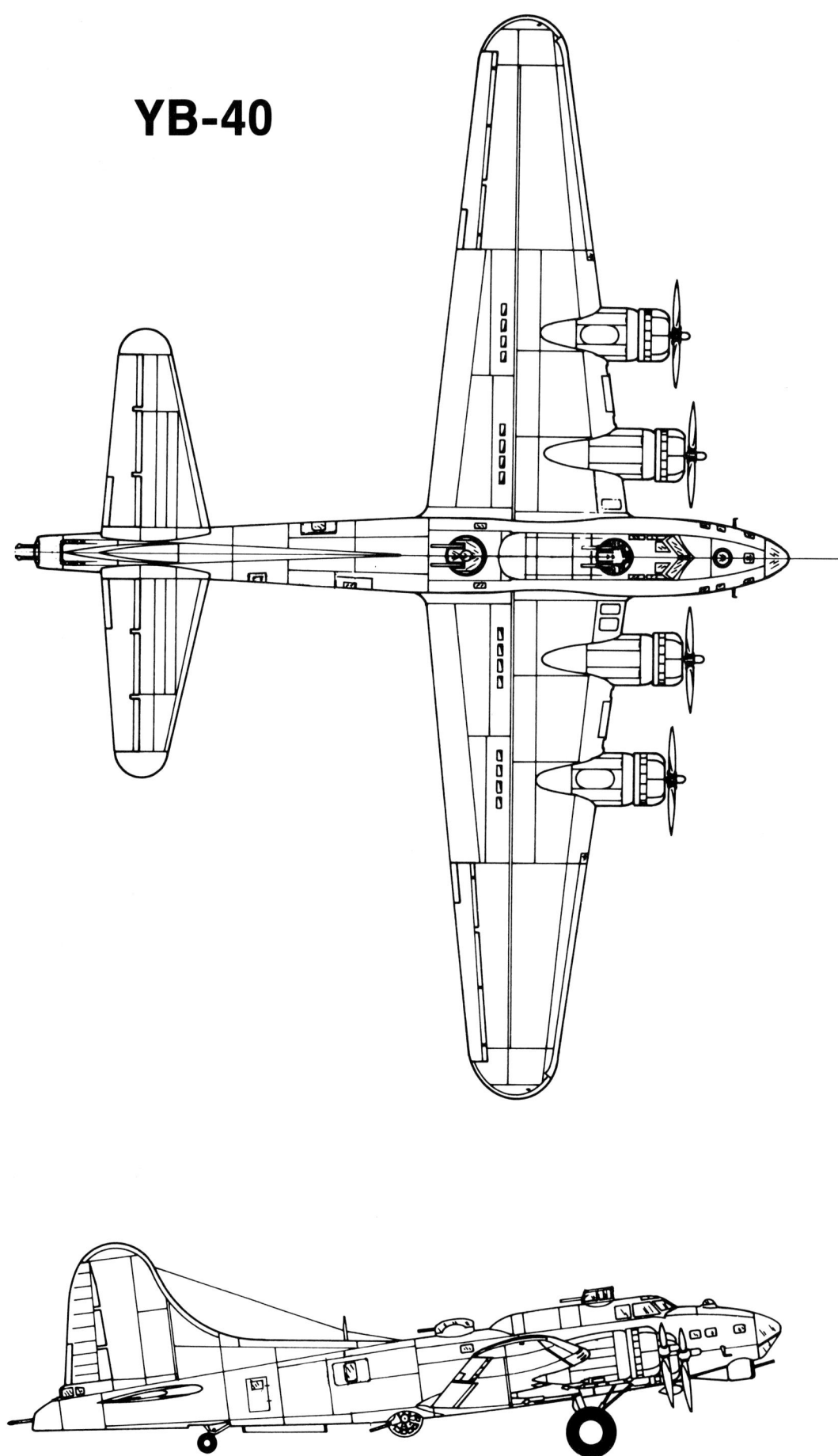

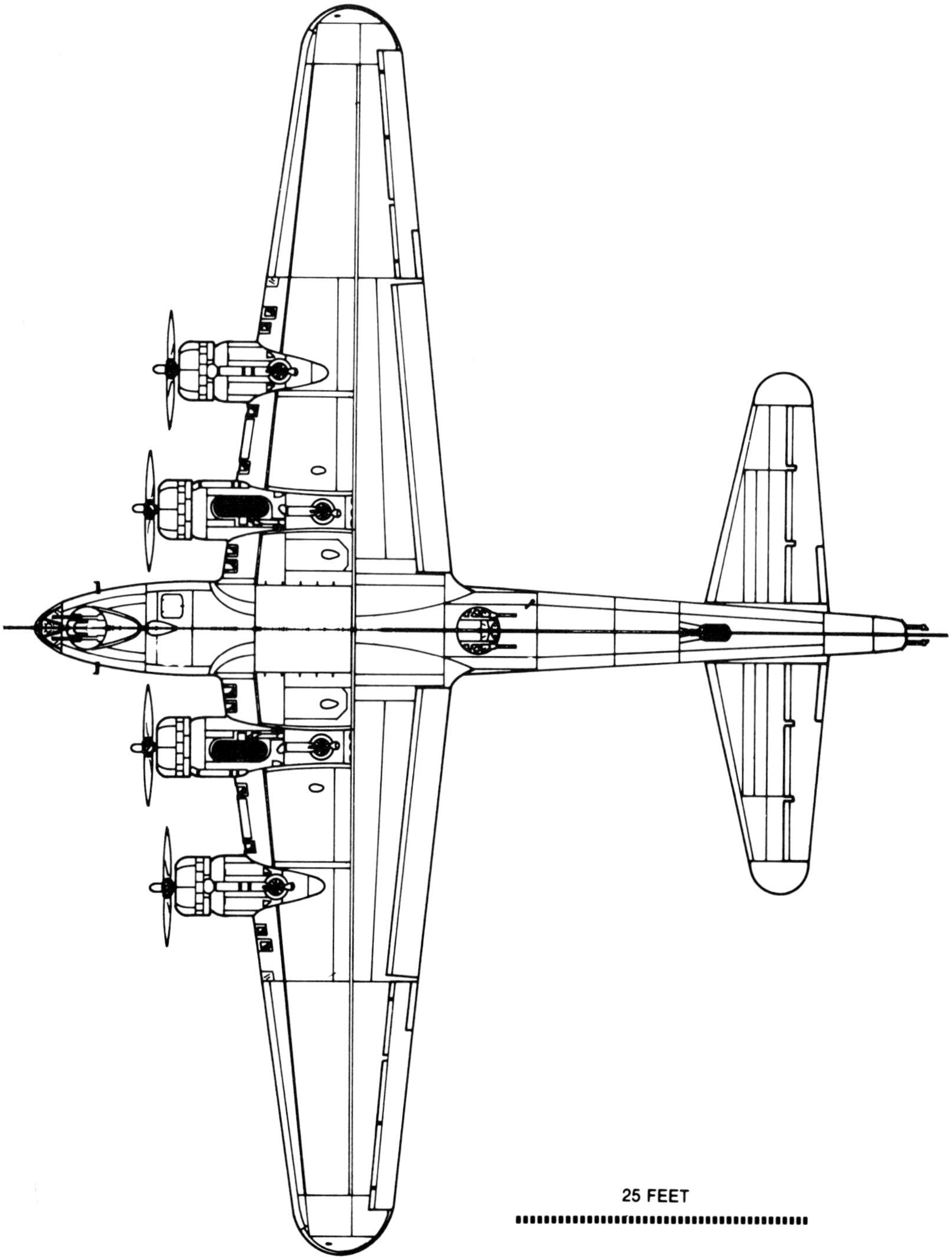

25 FEET

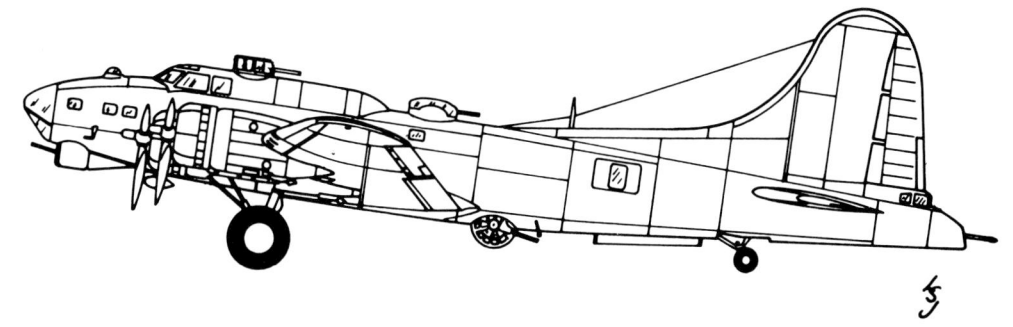

9

Table 2

AIRPLANE	POSITION	TOTAL CONSUMPTION	TOTAL TIME*	CONSUMPTION GAL./HR.
42-5742	No. 2 Leader 305th BG	1363 Gal.	6:00	227
42-5736	No. 2 Leader 92nd BG	1478 Gal.	6:05	245
	Low Sq. 92nd BG			
42-5737	No. 1 1st Element	1434 Gal.	6:00	240
42-5741	No. 2 1st Element	1025 Gal.	4:00	256
42-5744	No. 3 1st Element	1456 Gal.	6:40	218
42-5740	No. 1 2nd Element	1658 Gal.	6:30	256
42-5739	No. 2 2nd Element	1755 Gal.	7:00	250
42-5735	No. 3 2nd Element	1625 Gal.	6:30	250

* Total time includes both ground and air time.

Due to shortages of fuel, only three of the aircraft, 42-5742, 42-5736, and 42-5737, were able to return to Alconbury. Aircraft 42-5744 was able to attain such a low fuel consumption rate because it was flown using an auto lean mixture in all flight regimes except for the climb -- a condition deemed unwise for combat operations. It was recommended that the mission represented the maximum allowable range for the YB-40s without use of a bomb bay fuel tank.

The YB-40s experienced only one attack by enemy fighters. This attack was head on. The lead aircraft's chin turret fired a short burst and missed because the fighter did not press home his attack.

All of the chin and upper turrets functioned well during this first mission. One of the Sperry ball turrets experienced an electrical failure. The front guns on twelve out of sixteen twin USMC waist guns jammed due to the curvature of the ammunition feed chutes being too close to the guns. A hydraulic system failure resulted in a gunner having to operate his waist guns manually. Four charging handles on the tail guns broke due to inherent weaknesses. Weaknesses in the booster motor connections in the tail gun feed chutes resulted in cut out switch malfunctions. Another hydraulic system failure forced a tail gunner to operate his guns manually. All of the YB-40s were grounded from May 29 until June 15 to correct these armament deficiencies. The YB-40s had no difficulty maintaining formation with the B-17s. Power settings of 100 RPM less and 2 inches more of manifold pressure were used by the YB-40s than their companion B-17Fs.

On July 7, 1943, after nine missions, the commanding officer of the 92nd BG submitted a report to VIII Bomber Command citing numerous deficiencies in the armament systems on the YB-40s. The report also noted that there were no satisfactory ditching procedures for the aircraft. Recommendations in the report were that no additional YB-40s be sent to the theatre, future B-17s be equipped with the Bendix chin turrets, and that the waist gun positions be staggered on all B-17s.

Table 3

Date	Target	No. of YB-40s Dispatched	Remarks
29 May 1943	St. Nazaire	8	One YB-40 aborted.
15 June 1943	LeMans	4	Mission recalled due to weather.
22 June 1943	Huls	11	One YB-40 lost.
23 June 1943	LeMans	8	Mission recalled before reaching enemy coast.
25 June 1943	Hamburg	7	Two YB-40s aborted. Enemy a/c claimed: 2 destroyed, 1 damaged
26 June 1943	Paris	5	Enemy a/c claimed: 2 destroyed, 5 damaged, 1 probable
28 June 1943	St. Nazaire	6	Enemy a/c claimed: 1 destroyed, 1 damaged, 1 probable
29 June 1943	Paris	2	One YB-40 aborted.
4 July 1943	Nantes	1	
	LeMans	2	
14 July 1943	Villacoublay	5	
17 July 1943	Hannover	2	
24 July 1943	Heroya	1	
26 July 1943	Hannover	2	
28 July 1943	Kassel	2	

Table 4

XB/YB-40 Serial Number Data

XB-40

S/N	Remarks
41-24341	Originally the second B-17F-1-BO. Became a TB-40.

YB-40

S/N	Remarks
42-5732/42-5744	Originally B-17F-10-VE. All went to ETO with 327th BS, 92nd BG.
42-5871/42-5872	Originally B-17F-30-VE. Both became TB-40s.
42-5920/42-5921	Originally B-17F-35-VE. Both became TB-40s.
42-5923/42-5927	Originally B-17F-35-VE. All became TB-40s.

TB-40

S/N	Remarks
42-5833/42-5834	Originally B-17F-25-VE.

A total of fourteen missions were flown by the YB-40s between May and July 1943. Their success in repelling enemy fighters was only 10% greater than that of the B-17Fs, and this was attributed to the Bendix chin turret. The inability of the YB-40 to carry a bomb load was a further detriment. Carrying a load of ammunition into a target and out again, after the B-17s had dropped their bombs, caused the YB-40s to lag in formation and become a detriment to the formation. A summary of the YB-40 missions is shown in Table 3.

The battle for YB-40 program was alternately cancelled and reinstated until September 1943. In order to keep the program going, the Engineering Division at Wright Field suggested that the aircraft be service-evaluated in the Pacific, but this never came to pass.

YB-40, 42-5741 survived the war to serve as a trainer. The U-48 was a training number. This picture was taken at Ontario, California, in 1945. (G.S. Williams)

The Bendix chin turret installation on the XB-40 is shown here. An engineer uses the sighting control which would later appear on the B-17G. (Lockheed B1442)

Left side view of the Bendix chin turret installation on the XB-40. (Boeing P32349)

The data block indicates that aircraft 42-5741 was a TB-40. However, this ship went to England as a YB-40. The hot shot pilot was E.M. Grabowski. (USAF via E.M. Grabowski)

Twin .50 caliber USMC hydraulically-powered waist gun installation on the XB-40. *(Boeing P32351)*

The YB-40 had a staggered waist gun installation. (Compare with the photo at left of the XB-40.) As shown in this view, a total of eight .50 caliber guns could be brought to bear against the target. *(Douglas B-5983)*

Looking forward at the fuselage interior with the side guns stowed. The ball turret suspension system is visible. Note how the interior was unpainted. *(Douglas B-6430)*

Looking aft at the fuselage interior with the side guns in position. The vertical armor plate panels (dark) are clearly visible. The floor was plywood. The cylinder located in the aft fuselage was the toilet. *(Douglas B-6433)*

STAND-OFF WEAPONS CARRIERS

During and after World War II, a number of stand-off weapons were tested and used operationally on B-17s. Some of the weapons included razons, spazons, glide bombs, and JB-2s (equivalent to the German V-1 Buzz Bomb). Except for the JB-2s, the weapons were carried on bomb racks mounted between the inboard engines and the fuselage.

Above: B-17F-25-BO, 42-30921, was used as a mother ship for Buzz Bomb equipped B-17s at Wendover Field, Utah, during mid-1945. Note the additional antennas under the fuselage. (P.G. Mack)

A line up of Wendover-based B-17s during early 1945. The ships include B-17F-95-BO, 42-30234; B-17F-125-BO, 42-30921; and B-17F-40-BO, 42-5194. (P.G. Mack)

A B-17F takes off from Eglin Field with a pair of GB-1 glide bombs. (USAF)

A line up of glide bombs at Eglin Field on September 20, 1943. (USAF)

A pair of GB-1 glide bombs slung under a B-17E. The bombs were 1000 pounders. (USAF +32292AC)

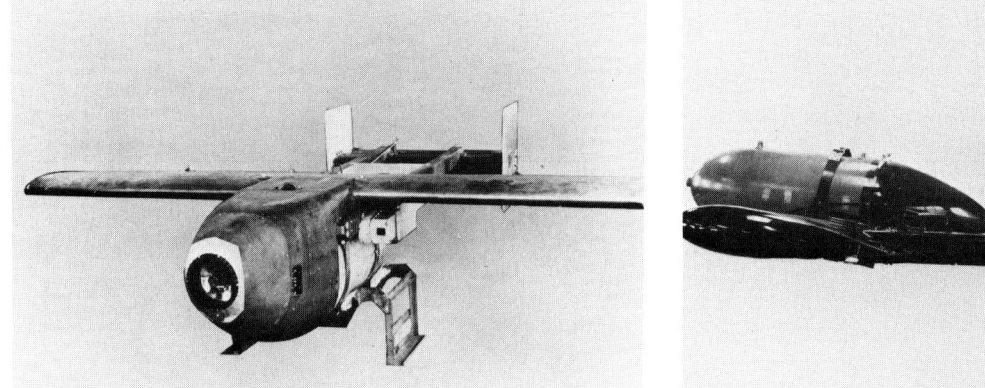
These two photos show two types of glide bombs carried by the B-17. (Left USAF £32291AC, right USAF 32290AC)

Torpedos also were rigged with wings and used as glide bombs. (USAF +31402AC)

A razon bomb carried by the B-17. Guidance control was afforded by the moveable tail fins. (USAF 31404AC)

JB-2 THUNDERBUG

A B-17G with a pair of JB-2 Thunderbugs mounted beneath the wings. (USAF 176362 via Boeing HS756)

A close-up of the JB-2 and its rack on a B-17G at Wendover Field. The cartoon with the "P.G." was for Phil Mack. (P.G. Mack)

B-17G-110-VE, 44-85815, with a JB-2 slung under the wing. (USAF via Boeing 104293)

Baby 9 was B-17G-90-DL, 44-83641, and it is seen here launching its second JB-2 in a test off Kwajalein in mid-1947 under "Project Sandstone". The aircraft was assigned to the 1st Guided Missile Group at Eglin, and operated on detached service under JTF-7. (H.T. Ward)

BQ-7s
APHRODITE, BATTY, & CASTOR

Mugwump had first served with the 100th BG and then the 96th BG before joining the Aphrodite program. (USAF)

The Germans had mounted their V-1 assault against London in mid-June 1944. These flying bombs were launched from sites in the Pas de Calais area of France. For the 8th Air Force in England, these became known as No-Ball targets. Intense anti-aircraft activity was encountered at these targets.

To counter the V-1 threat, Project Aphrodite was initiated under the code name Weary Willy. Tests were begun at the Air Force's Proving Ground in Florida using war weary B-17s. In late-June 1944 Project Aphrodite was begun in England. Ten war-weary B-17Fs and Gs were stripped of all armament and other equipment resulting in a 32,000-pound weight savings. A double Azon radio system was coupled to the autopilot system. Then a load of boxed explosives was distributed between the flight deck, bomb bay, and radio compartments. The weight distribution was as follows:

Basic Weight	32,000 lbs
Crew Weight	200
Oil Weight	600
Forward Payload	6,500
Bomb Bay Payload	18,500
Radio Compartment Payload	6,500
Gross Weight	64,300 lbs

The ordnance layer was as shown in the following figure.

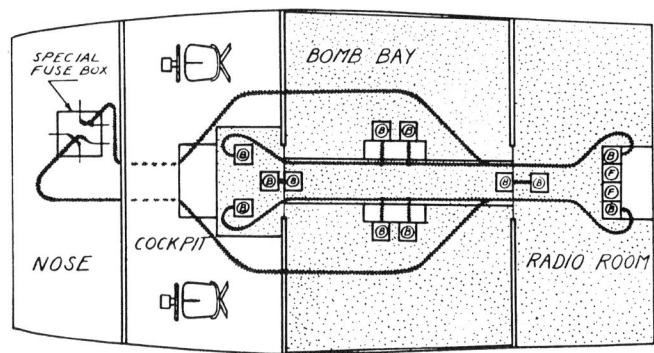

The "baby" ships carried a crew of two -- a pilot and an autopilot technician. When launched on a mission, the "baby's" pilot would fly the aircraft while the technician stabilized the autopilot and positive control was gained by the "mother" ship. Then the technician would bail out, followed by the pilot. A static line was rigged to the main backpack parachute. A reserve chest pack was also worn by the crewmen. The "mother" ship would then attempt to direct the drone to the target. The results of Project Aphrodite were insignificant.

APHRODITE

LTC Roy Forrest was photographed in the cockpit of the "Roadster" with its cut down upper decking. The upper surfaces of the aircraft were overpainted in a scalloped white for visibility. (Boeing HS 909)

The "Roadster" cockpit. Only one ship was so modified.
(USAF Museum A1/B-17/Pho 65)

A view of the "Roadster's" faired over upper fuselage.
(Boeing HS 910)

The remote throttle controls for an Aphrodite ship are shown here. (USAF)

Right side view of the "Roadster's" cockpit. (USAF Museum A1/B-17/Pho 25)

APHRODITE SHIPS

S/N	Block No.	Name	Code	Former/Group Station
42-30342	B-17F-100-BO	Taint A Bird	BG-G	95th/334th
42-37760	B-17G-10-DL	-	VE-F	381st/532nd
42-30595	B-17F-110-BO	Gremlin Gus II	K	388th
42-3461	B-17F-65-DL	-	PY-S	92nd/407th
41-24639	B-17F-27-BO	The Careful Virgin	OR-W	91st/323rd
42-31394	B-17G-15-BO	-	LF-?	379th/526th
42-3440	B-17F-60-DL	-	SU-B	384th/544th
42-39835	B-17G-1-VE	Wantta Spar	TU-N	351st/510th
42-6080	B-17F-45-VE	Wewa Special	OE-P	95th/325th
42-3493	B-17F-70-DL	-	NV-H	92nd/325th

BATTY

B-17G-10-VE, s/n 42-40043, control ship with the Batty GB-4 glide bombs. (USAF)

Project Batty was still another attempt at remote operations. B-17G-10-VE, s/n 42-40043, was modified to carry a pair of radio controlled GB-4 glide bombs. The modified 2,000 lb. bombs weighed 2,600 lbs. They had 12 foot wings installed. A pair of booms held a tail section. The overall length of the GB-4 was twelve feet, two inches. Five magnesium flares were fitted to the tail section for viewing by the TV camera in the "mother" ship. After three tests, the B-17 made two operational missions. One was to the port of Le Harve on August 13, 1944, and the second was to La Palice on August 26, 1944. The state-of-the-art for control was not sufficient and both missions were unsuccessful.

A deHavilland Mosquito, s/n MM370, formates with Batty-quipped B-17G-10-VE, s/n 42-40043. A pair of Batty GB-4 glide bombs were hung under the B-17, and are just discernable under the fuselage. (USAF)

CASTOR

This drone control ship, B-17G-75-B, s/n 43-37953, reveals its control receiving antenna (1), which is a whip antenna, and Rebecca/Eureka antenna (2). (USAF)

***Ten Knights in a Barroom**, formerly of the 95th BG, with her mission markers and kill marks. This view reveals the removed crew hatch and new hatch spoiler, smoke tank, and TV antenna under the nose.* (USAF)

Project Castor was the follow-on program. In addition to the double Azon modifications on the Aphrodite ships, an RC-487 television transmitter was installed on the drones. An Eureka AN/TPN-1 radio beacon system was also installed. The Rebecca AN/APN-2 airborne interrogator (IFF forerunner) installed on the "mother" ships tracked the Eureka transmissions.

A 75-gallon drop tank was modified into a smoke generator and installed on the bomb bay doors of the "baby" ships. This device was controllable from the "mother" ship and was used to improve visibility of the "baby" or drone ship.

The Castor drones were loaded with 21,000 lbs. of boxes containing 18,425 lbs. of torpex. The boxes were distributed as follows: 25 on the flight deck, 210 in the bomb bay, and 100 in the radio compartment. The drone pilot would arm the load before bailing out of the ship.

APHRODITE AND CASTOR MISSIONS

Date	Aircraft	Target
4 Aug 1944	42-30342	Watten
4 Aug 1944	42-39835	Siracourt
4 Aug 1944	42-3461	Wizernes
4 Aug 1944	41-24639	Mimoyecques
6 Aug 1944	42-30212	Watten
6 Aug 1944	42-31394	Watten
11 Sep 1944	42-30180	Heligoland
14 Sep 1944	42-30363	Hemmingstedt
14 Sep 1944	42-39827	Hemmingstedt
15 Oct 1944	42-30039	Heligoland
15 Oct 1944	42-37743	Heligoland
30 Oct 1944	42-30066	Heligoland
30 Oct 1944	42-3432	Heligoland
5 Dec 1944	42-39824	Herford
5 Dec 1944	42-30353	Herford
1 Jan 1945	42-30178	Oldenburg
1 Jan 1945	42-30237	Oldenburg

This view of the aircraft shown above right, shows the new nose antenna and smoke tank sway brace. (USAF)

The Rebecca transmitting whip antenna was located aft of the "mother" ship's radio compartment. (USAF)

The Eureka transponder in a drone ship. (USAF)

A Rebecca scope on a B-17 drone control ship. (USAF)

The forward right corner of a control ship radio compartment. (USAF)

Side view of the smoke tank and the smoke generators. The tank was a modified 75 gallon fuel tank. (USAF)

Aft lower view of the smoke tank showing smoke generators and sway brace. (USAF)

TV receiving antenna on the tail of a drone control ship. (USAF)

TV transmitting antenna on the tail of a Castor ship. (USAF)

CASTOR SHIPS

S/N	Block No.	Name	Code	Former Group/Squadron
42-30212	B-17F-90-BO	Quarterback	-	888th
42-30180	B-17F-90-BO	Guzzlers	-	96th
42-30363	B-17F-100-BO	Ruth L III	-	96th
42-39827	B-17G-1-VE	-	-	306th
42-30039	B-17F-85-BO	Liberty Belle	-	384th
42-37743	B-17G-10-DL	-	-	94th
42-30066	B-17F-85-BO	Mugwump	X	388th
42-3438	B-17F-60-DL	-	-	96th
42-39824	B-17G-1-VE	-	-	-
42-30353	B-17F-100-BO	Ten Knights in a Barroom	OE-Z	95th/335th
42-30178	B-17G-90-BO	Darlin' Dolly	-	95th
42-30237	B-17F-95-BO	Stump Jumper	WA-V	379th/524th

PHOTO-RECON B-17s

Shutterbug, *was B-17F-125-BO, 42-30981. This aircraft was undergoing cold weather tests in Alaska during 1943-1944. (170086 USAF)*

As a stop-gap measure in meeting the reconnaissance needs in the Pacific and Mediterranean Theatres, several early B-17s received temporary field modifications to accept aerial cameras. These aircraft retained their B-17 designations. Subsequently, the USAAF developed true photo-reconnaissance versions of the B-17 as follows: sixteen F-9s, twenty-five F-9A/F-9Bs, and ten F-9Cs. Cameras were installed in the nose and the bomb bay/radio compartment. A trimetrogon mount was installed in the nose. Various camera combinations were carried amidships. The F-9, F-9A, and F-9B were derived from B-17Fs, whereas the F-9C evolved from the B-17G. Specific camera installations differentiated these aircraft types. Basically, the F-9s cruised at 260 mph at 28,000 feet, and had a 2,000-mile range.

In the photo-reconnaissance role, the F-9s suffered heavily to enemy fighter action while flying alone. High loss rates surprised American planners, and the aircraft were subsequently relegated to the less dangerous photo-mapping role.

The prototype F-9C, S/N 43-37914, was developed at the United Air Lines Modification Center, Cheyenne, Wyoming, between April 4 and November 9, 1944. Camera installations were developed to ensure that there was no masking of the photographic image by the camera windows or any object within the fuselage. Masking due to structure outside of the fuselage was kept to an absolute minimum. Revisions to the standard aircraft equipment as required to enhance the photographic performance had a negligable effect on the structural and aerodynamic performance of the aircraft.

Each multi-camera installation was provided with a single, integral mount which was shockmounted to the supporting structure. The chin turret was replaced by a trimetrogon mount for three six inch K-17 or K-17B cameras. In the radio compartment, provisions were made for installation of a single vertical K-17, K-18, K-19, K-22, or similar camera with a focal length ranging from six inches to forty inches. Radio compartment provisions were also made for a pair of K-17 or K-22 cameras with twelve, twenty-four, or forty inch lenses mounted in a split vertical installation with a right and left oblique allowing a one inch overlap in photographic image.

Dual camera controls were provided, one in the nose, and the other in the rear camera bay. The panels were wired so that any combination of cameras could be operated from either location. An A-2 viewfinder was installed at each camera control area.

All current navigation equipment was retained. The bombsight was tied in with the autopilot and a C-1 pilot director was installed. In addition to the standard radio equipment, an SCR-718 radio altimeter was installed.

A pair of Janitrol 50,000 BTU gasoline heaters were added, one in the nose and the other in the rear camera bay. Ducting was installed to allow hot air to flow directly across each camera window for defrosting. In addition, the hot air warmed the cameras and surrounding area. Canvas boots completely sealed the camera wells.

Except for the chin turret, all existing armament remained. The aircraft center of gravity was not affected. Firing tests proved that no blast tubes were required on the guns in order to protect the camera windows.

Sufficient oxygen was carried to permit a minimum endurance of eight hours at 30,000 feet. Using two bomb bay fuel tanks, a maximum of 3,600 gallons of gasoline could be carried in order to maximize the range of the aircraft.

The F-9 development began in mid-1942. F-9s, which were developed from B-17Fs, were redesignated FB-17Fs in 1945, and then changed to RB-17Fs in 1948. F-9Cs, derived from B-17Gs, were reidentified as FB-17Gs in 1945, and then redesignated as RB-17Gs in 1948.

This Y1B-17 served as a reconnaissance aircraft with the 38th RS, 19th BG when they were stationed at Albuquerque, New Mexico, the second half of 1941. The black and yellow checkered cowls were indicative of the reconnaissance squadron (the bombardment squadrons had solid colored cowls). The 38R on the tail was for the 38th RS. The number 33 for the individual aircraft number appeared on the fin and was repeated on the nose. The squadron insignia appeared on the nose. With the beginning of World War II, the recon squadrons were no longer attached to the bomb groups. The 38th RS and this insignia were transferred to the 427th BS and assigned to the 303rd BG. This particular aircraft was subsequently painted olive drab and gray at a depot and flown from Hamilton Field to Hickam on December 7, 1941. This aircraft is believed to have carried the number 49, and it crashed at Bellows Field. *(USAF via W. Cleveland)*

Arctic Queen *was an F-9C operated in Alaska. By outward appearances the aircraft would have been s/n 44-83497. The top turret was removed, and an extra astrodome appears in the turret position along with an ADF loop antenna.* *(via P.M. Bowers)*

A view showing the 91st RS flight line. An SB-17G appears second in the line up. *(USAF)*

Serial Number Data

Type	S/N	Previous Type
F-9-DL	42-3324	B-17F-45-DL
F-9-VE	42-5753	B-17F-15-VE
F-9-BO	42-29676	B-17F-65-BO
F-9-BO	42-29719	B-17F-65-BO
F-9-BO	42-29753	B-17F-70-BO
F-9-BO	42-29783	B-17F-70-BO
F-9-BO	42-29801	B-17F-70-BO
F-9-BO	42-29805	B-17F-70-BO
F-9-BO	42-30083	B-17F-85-BO
F-9-BO	42-30220	B-17F-90-BO
F-9-BO	42-30232	B-17F-95-BO
F-9-BO	42-30252	B-17F-95-BO
F-9-BO	42-30268	B-17F-95-BO
F-9-BO	42-30299	B-17F-95-BO
F-9-BO	42-30253	B-17F-95-BO
F-9A-DL	42-2984	B-17F-10-DL
F-9A-VE	42-6129	B-17F-50-VE
F-9A-VE	42-6134	B-17F-50-VE
F-9A-VE	42-6135	B-17F-50-VE
F-9A-VE	42-6138	B-17F-50-VE
F-9A-VE	42-6140	B-17F-50-VE
F-9A-VE	42-6159	B-17F-50-VE
F-9A-VE	42-6164	B-17F-50-VE
F-9A-VE	42-6283/42-6187	B-17F-50-VE
F-9A-VE	42-6200/42-6201	B-17F-50-VE
F-9A-BO	42-29873	B-17F-75-BO
F-9A-BO	42-29899	B-17F-75-BO
F-9A-BO	42-29902	B-17F-75-BO
F-9A-BO	42-29904	B-17F-75-BO
F-9A-BO	42-29911	B-17F-75-BO
F-9A-BO	42-29913	B-17F-75-BO
F-9A-BO	42-29922	B-17F-75-BO
F-9A-BO	42-30469	B-17F-105-BO
F-9A-BO	42-30486	B-17F-105-BO
F-9B-DL		F-9A-DL
F-9B-VE		F-9A-DL
F-9B-BO		F-9A-BO
F-9C-BO	43-37689	B-17G-70-BO
F-9C-BO	43-37711	B-17G-70-BO
F-9C-BO	43-37914	B-17G-75-BO
F-9C-BO	43-38155	B-17G-80-BO
F-9C-BO	43-38162	B-17G-80-BO
F-9C-BO	43-38168	B-17G-80-BO
F-9C-BO	43-38649	B-17G-90-BO
F-9C-BO	43-38651	B-17G-90-BO
F-9C-BO	43-38653	B-17G-90-BO
F-9C-DL	44-83626	B-17G-90-DL

Trimetrogon camera chin installation. This fairing was installed in lieu of the chin turret and fairing on the B-17G when converted to an F-9C. (NASM 80-15406)

Trimetrogon chin fairing on F-9C-75-BO, 43-37914. A heater air scoop was added just forward of the crew entry hatch. (NASM 80-15405)

The C-1 pilot director was installed where the navigator's astrodome was normally located. (NASM 80-15420)

The C-1 pilot director as viewed from the inside of the aircraft. (NASM 80-15419)

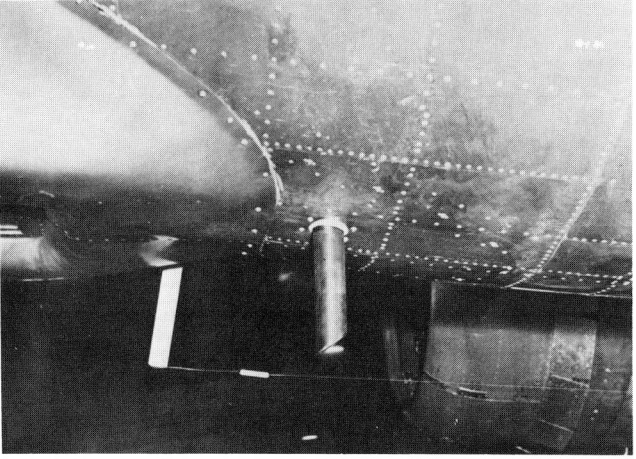

A drift meter tube was located aft of the chin fairing. (NASM 80-15424)

The rear camera bay heater air scoop was located on the right side of the fuselage just aft of the wing root fairing and ahead of the waist window. (NASM 80-15416)

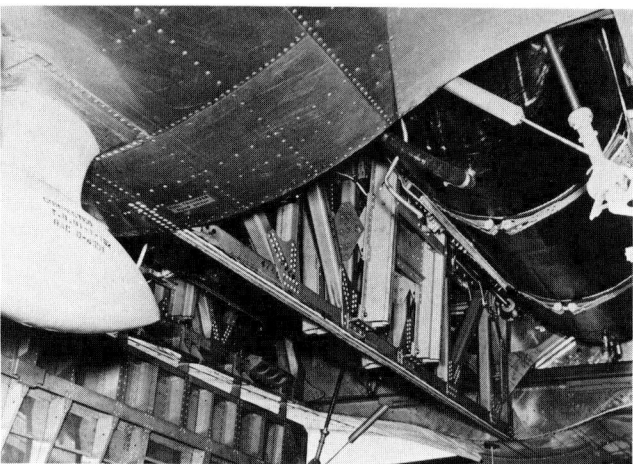

The ADF loop antenna was located just forward of the bomb bay. A pair of auxiliary fuel tanks was installed in the bomb bay. (NASM 80-15413)

The aft camera bay was located just forward of the ball turret. The camera bay doors are shown open in this view. A spoiler, located just forward of the camera bay, kept debris (bugs etc.) from impinging on the camera window. (NASM 80-15414)

Heater ducting was located on the left side of the forward fuselage. (NASM 80-15412)

View showing the heater ducting located on the right side of the fuselage just above the ball turret. (NASM 80-15418)

The aft camera bay doors are shown here in the closed position. (NASM 80-15415)

The trimetrogon camera mount was installed in the space normally occupied by the chin turret. (NASM 80-15407)

A-2 view finders were located in both the forward and aft camera bays. (NASM 80-15422)

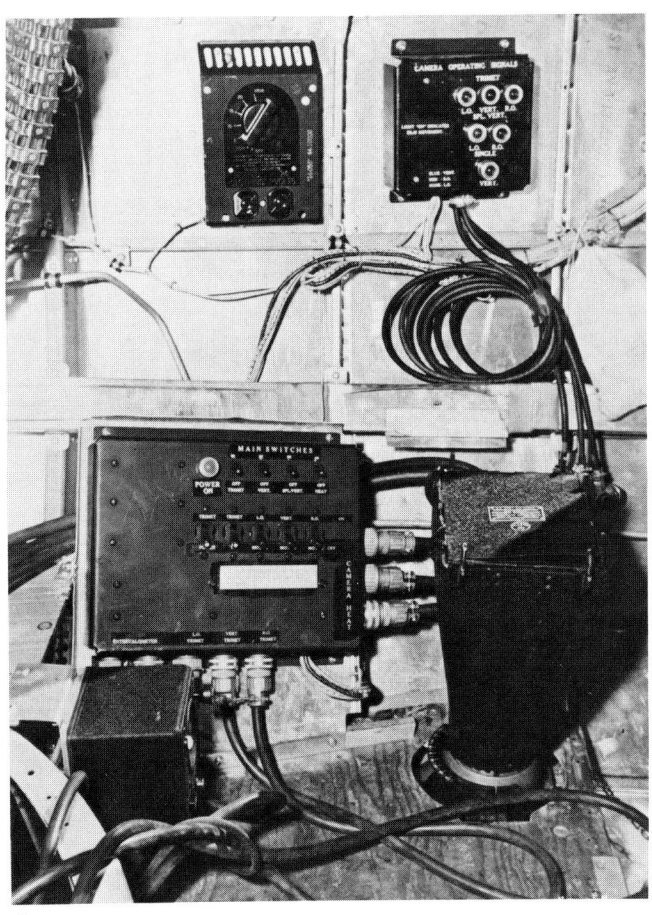

Camera controls as they appeared in the forward camera bay. (NASM 80-15409)

The aft camera bay interior. (NASM 80-15410)

PROJECT REED

Dreamboat, *B-17E, 41-9112, with Project Reed modifications. A short-lived red surround to the national insignia dates the photograph to the June-August 1943 time frame. The nose art is visible.* (NASM)

Early loss rates in the 8th Air Force in England were not acceptable, and efforts were made to reduce them. Both tactics and equipment were reviewed and revised to meet the Luftwaffe threat. Local commanders took it upon themselves to make certain field modifications in order to improve the defensive firepower on their aircraft.

One such modification is covered here. It was accomplished by the 92nd BG under the direction of Major Robert J. Reed. B-17E, 41-9112, named **Dreamboat** was selected for the project.

Numerous armament changes were made to the aircraft. They were as follows:
- Consolidated hydraulically-powered turrets (the same as those used on the B-24), were added to nose and tail. The nose gunner was separated from the bombardier.
- A powered twin .50 caliber gun installation was added to the radio compartment. These guns could traverse a 180° azimuth, 78° elevation and 45° depression. This installation was to replace the waist positions. With the incorporation of this change, the crew could be reduced from ten to eight.
- An external ammunition supply was provided for the ball turret, thereby affording the gunner more room. In addition to improving crew comfort, the gunner was then able to wear a backpack parachute.
- The Sperry top turret was replaced by a Martin turret (like that used on the B-26). This turret was 120 pounds lighter, took up less space in the cockpit, and offered a seat for the gunner.

Non-armament changes to the aircraft were:
- The bombardier and navigator duties were combined and served by a single crewmember.
- The bombardier station was located in a gondola under the nose.
- The radio compartment was moved forward to the nose, thereby improving the aircraft center of gravity, and greatly enhancing communication with the navigator.
- The radio operator also served as the nose gunner.
- Bi-fold bomb bay doors replaced the standard doors. This change reduced drag and improved the ball turret gunner's vision.
- The single HF antenna wire running from the waist (radio compartment) to the fin was replaced by a nose-to-fin-to-right-wingtip antenna. This change increased the radio signal.
- A rerouted redundant oxygen system was installed. This new system offered greater protection against battle damage and provided a back-up.

All of these changes resulted in a 1,000 pound lighter airframe with improved handling characteristics. Notwithstanding, there was no speed advantage over the production B-17Fs due to the lack of streamlining on the Reed modifications.

This ship was flown to 8th AF bomber bases for review and comment. German intelligence thought that this aircraft was a B-40 modification with no less than twenty-five guns.

None of the Reed changes were incorporated in production because late B-17Fs and the new B-17Gs were already on the production line. In addition, the B-29 was destined to replace the B-17.

The considerable changes to the forward fuselage are evident in this photo. (NASM)

Changes to the top turret, radio compartment and tail turret are revealed in this view. (NASM)

The Consolidated tail turret, radio compartment guns and flatter Martin top turret may be seen here. (NASM)

The considerable nose modifications are shown in this view. The nose had been faired to accommodate the Consolidated turret. A gondola was added for the bombardier. The bomb-aiming panel had a windshield wiper, and a pitot probe was installed under the nose. The normal pitot probe was moved up (like for the B-24) and it also served as a mast for the new HF antenna. An insulator for the antenna lead appears beneath the windows. The open crew hatch door extends beneath the gondola. *(NASM)*

Above left: The lower portion of the bombardier's gondola is shown in this view. The bi-fold bomb bay doors extended a mere eight inches beneath the fuselage instead of the normal thirty-two inches. *(NASM)*

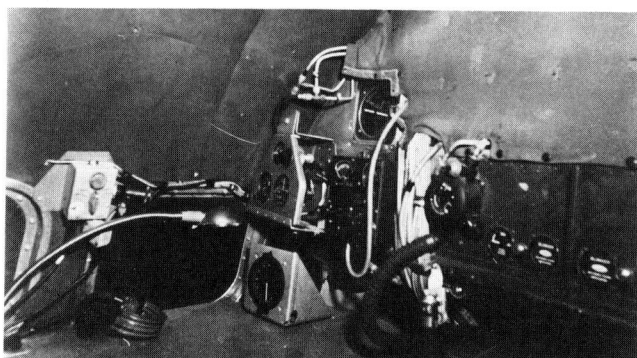

The radio operator's station was located within the nose. *(NASM)*

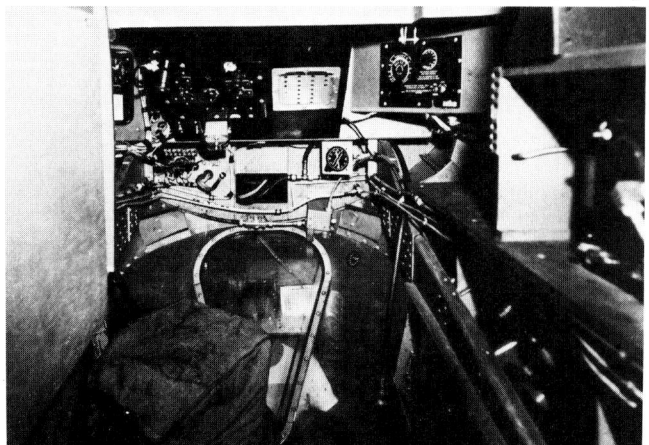

This view looks forward and down into the bombardier's station. The Norden bomb sight is covered. *(NASM)*

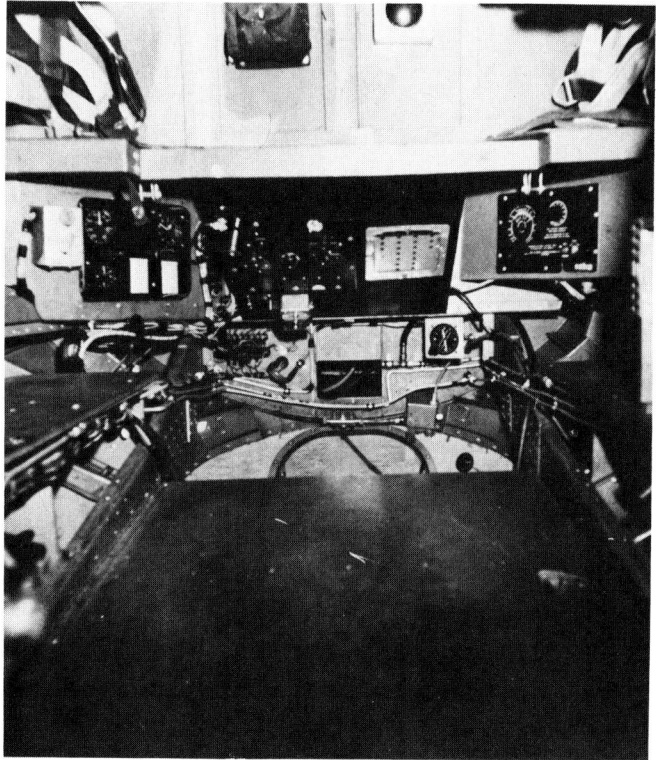

This view looks forward into the bombardier's station. *(NASM)*

COLOR GALLERY

TB-40, s/n 42-5927. This aircraft has training numbers, 253, on the nose and fin. A Vega cartoon is barely discernable on the waist. (USAF K3365)

RB-17G from the 6204th Photo Mapping Flight (Provisional) is shown during an engine runup while sitting runway alert. This photo was taken in January 1951 at Clark AB, Philippines. Ten mission markers were painted on the nose. (Biteman via W. Thompson)

ALL WEATHER FLYING CENTER

Above: The All Weather Flying Center operated a variety of aircraft. In addition to this TB-17, a pair of P-47s and a C-82 are visible. The B-17 was still armed. (J. Vollemeck)

Left: An All Weather Flying Center TB-17G undergoing engine maintenance. (J. Vollemeck)

Below: The nose markings cut through the crew entry hatch on this All Weather Flying Center B-17. (J. Vollemeck)

CLANDESTINE OPERATIONS

Above: TB-17G-95-VE, s/n 44-85531, at Clark AB in October 1957. This ship was used for clandestine operations.   (Picciani Aircraft Slides)

Right: This close-up of 44-85531 reveals the additional antennas on the nose and the exhaust suppressors.
(Picciani Aircraft Slides)

Ex-B-17G-95-DL, s/n 44-83785, carried civil registry N809Z. This aircraft had an aerial pick-up device mounted in the nose.
(W.T. Larkins via G.S. Williams)

This view of N809Z shows three windows in the waist and an escape chute in the tail. The chute was used to drop agents.   (W.T. Larkins via G.S. Williams)

This head-on view of N809Z reveals the pick-up gear and the open doors in the bottom of the nose compartment through which the retrieved person was recovered.
(W.T. Larkins via G.S. Williams)

DRONE B-17s

DB-17P-105-BO, s/n 43-39155. This aircraft had a black belly and a walkway along the wing root.
(R.E. Clark via D. Menard)

Right side view of 43-39155 shown in the photo above.
(R.E. Clark via D. Menard)

Drone TB-17G-85-DL, s/n 44-83560, of the 58th BW, landing at Stickell Field, Eniwetok Island. (USAF K15861)

Drone TB-17G-90-DL, s/n 44-83603, of the 58th BW, was used in the Bikini A-bomb tests. The outboard wing panels and tail section were insignia yellow, as was the spacing between the black waist bands.
(USAF K15839)

This QB-17N is shown landing at Eglin AFB. The aircraft was overall day-glo orange with black lettering. The anti-glare panels were black. The fabric control surfaces were left in silver so as not to have to rebalance them. (G.S. Williams)

Drone Control TB-17G-110-VE, s/n 44-85818. The large AS-154/APS-10 antenna fairing is well defined in this view. (USAF K4440)

TB-17G-110-VE, s/n 44-85820 from the 58th BW as photographed at Wright Field. This aircraft served as a drone during the Bikini atomic bomb tests. (Cavenaugh via D. Menard)

This rare photograph shows a historic moment for Boeing and the USAF. This is a single frame taken from a movie camera at great distance, and it shows the last B-17 operated by the Air Force being used as a drone target for a Boeing Bomarc surface-to-air missile. A split second after this photo was taken, the missile destroyed the B-17, and the Air Force would never again operate a Flying Fortress. The event was significant to Boeing in that Boeing built both the B-17 and the Bomarc missile. (Boeing SA14208)

This borate bomber, N66573, was B-17G-85-DL, s/n 44-83585. She was known as the **Batmobile,** and was lost in a box canyon while fighting a fire at Cayuse Saddle, Montana, in 1979. (G.S. Williams)

Another view of the **Batmobile.** (G.S. Williams)

N9323Z was B-17G-85-DL, s/n 44-83514. The aircraft was operated by Aero Unia of Chino, California.
(W.T. Larkins via G.S. Williams)

With Mexican registry XB-BOE, this aircraft was B-17G-95-DL, s/n 44-83864, and had also served the US Navy as PB-1W, BuNo 77232. *(W.T. Larkins via G.S. Williams)*

HK580 was operated by the Columbian government. The slit windows were put in for the passengers who were prisoners being flown to a remote jungle prison. *(G.S. Williams)*

This photomapping B-17G was photographed at Barr Flood, Port Moresby, New Guinea, in 1967. With French registry F-BEEA, this was B-17G-100-VE, s/n 44-85643. *(W. Mathewes via G.S. Williams)*

RESTORED B-17s

The restored B-17G of the Confederate Air Force is shown taxiing with the Texas flag displayed above the nose. This photo was taken in September 1977. (Kinzey)

The same aircraft as seen above is shown here one year earlier in a different paint scheme. (Kinzey)

This close-up of the nose shows a circular plate over the location for the chin turret, and indicates that the aircraft is a former B-17G. **Texas Raiders** appears on the nose. (Kinzey)

Beautifully restored B-17G **Sentimental Journey** is shown here as it appeared in October 1979. (Bossie)

These two B-17Gs are owned by the Royal Air Force Museum. They are authentically marked to represent the 351st BG, 1st AD, 8th AF (triangle J), and the 94th BG, 3rd AD, 8th AF (square A). (Pealing via Jury)

OPERATION CROSSROADS

A line-up of the four drone ships shows the placement of the tail markings. This photo was taken in the U.S. prior to the aircraft deploying for Operation Crossroads. *(USAF)*

The 509th Composite Group dropped the only atomic weapons during wartime when they struck Hiroshima and Nagasaki in 1945. With the end of the war came a dramatic reduction in manning and operational capability of the U.S. Army Air Forces. By January 1946, the 509th Composite Group, residing at Roswell, New Mexico, could barely keep their aircraft in the air for routine pilot proficiency. The only remaining asset was their knowledge of atomic weapons.

On January 10, 1946, Col. P.T. Cullen was tasked with preparing the 509th Composite Group for Operation Crossroads. The Group was assigned to Vice Admiral W.H.P. Blandy's Task Force 1. By April 15, 1946, the 509th was to be manned, equipped, trained and operationally ready for their mission. The date for the actual atomic bomb drop test had been scheduled for May 15. However, it was delayed until July 1st.

The following U.S. Army Air Forces aircraft were assigned to the project:
- One B-29 command aircraft
- One B-29 bomb carrying aircraft **(Dave's Dream)**
- Two B-29 pressure drop aircraft
- Three B-29 weather reconnaissance aircraft
- Two B-29 (F-13) VLR radiological reconnaissance aircraft
- Eight F-13 VLR photographic aircraft
- Two C-54 photographic aircraft
- Four B-17 drone aircraft
- Five B-17 drone control aircraft
- Eleven B-17H (SB-17G) dumbos (if available from CinCPacUSA)
- One B-29 radio broadcast aircraft
- One B-29 press photography aircraft
- Two C-54 observation aircraft

A number of naval ships and aircraft were also provided for the project but are outside the scope of this publication.

A wide variety of special mission instrumentation was added to the various aircraft. Modifications to the B-17 drones and drone controllers were as follows:

B-17 DRONE AIRCRAFT	
EQUIPMENT	USE
AN/ARW-1 (Control)	Open and closes Air Sampler Bag equipment in addition to normal use.
SCR-718 (Altimeter)	Normal
SCR-522 (VHF)	Transmits Geiger Counter warning.
SCR-274-N (Command)	On two (2) Drones will be auto-keyed for propagation tests. Remains silent on other two (2).
BC-375 (Liaison)	Auto-keyed on all Drones to aid location by control aircraft.
AN/APT-5 (Jamming)	On one (1) Drone only. Transmits for propagation tests.

Drone ship four in flight with drone control ship V. *(USAF via Boeing HS-894)*

Drone Control ship III lifts off from Stickell Field, Eniwetok Island. *(USAF via Boeing)*

*This right side view of drone 1 reveals the yellow empannage color and single tail stripe and waist band. The ship carried the name **Super Spare** on the nose.* (W. Bodie via G.S. Williams)

B-17 DRONE CONTROL AIRCRAFT

EQUIPMENT	USE
AN/ARW-18 (Control)	Opens and closes air sampler bag on Drones in addition to normal use.
AN/AXR-1 (Television)	To be equipped with camera to record transmission from Drone.
AN/APN-9 (Loran)	Normal.
SCR-718 (Altimeter)	Do.
AN/ARN-7 (Compass)	1. Homes on BC-375 (liaison) in Drones. 2. Navigation by means of two (2) beacons on 260 KCS and 300 KCS.
SCR-522 (VHF)	Normal.
VHF Receiver (1st Extra)	Guards 140.58 MCS at all times.
VHF Receiver (2nd Extra)	Receives Geiger Counter warning from Drones.
SCR-274-N (Command)	Normal.
BC-375 (Liaison Transmitter).	Used by radiological observer.
AN/APR-4 RCM AN/ARR-5 Search AN/ARR-7 Receives	Two (2) aircraft will be equipped to monitor communications frequencies and two (2) aircraft will be equipped to monitor radar frequencies. Particular attention will be paid to emissions from the Drone aircraft.

Specific markings were prescribed for the task force aircraft. The B-17s all carried the 58th BW insignia on both sides of the nose. Black Roman numerals were carried on the tails of the five drone control aircraft. A set of black horizontal tail stripes and broad black waist bands were carried on the four drone aircraft, with the number of stripes corresponding to the number of bands. In addition, insignia yellow paint was applied to the outboard wing panels, tail section, and between the waist bands on the drone aircraft. The waist bands were twenty-four inches wide.

The aircraft identification for the B-17s were as follows:

Drone Aircraft

1	B-17G-85-DL	44-83560
2	B-17G-85-DL	44-83553
3	B-17G-90-DL	44-83603
4	B-17G-85-DL	44-83519

Drone Control Aircraft

I	B-17G-110-VE	44-85818
II	B-17G-110-VE	44-85815
III	B-17G-105-VE	44-85752
IV	B-17G-105-VE	44-85738
V	B-17G-100-VE	44-85690

Drone control ship I reveals AS-154/APS-10 antenna fairing on the belly. It measured 61"x36"x24" (LxWxD). On January 13, 1947, this ship controlled another B-17 in a flight from Eglin Field, Florida, to the HQ Air Proving Ground Command field in Washington, D.C. The "beeper" pilot flew both ships through a weather front and a practice bombing run.
(USAF 32667)

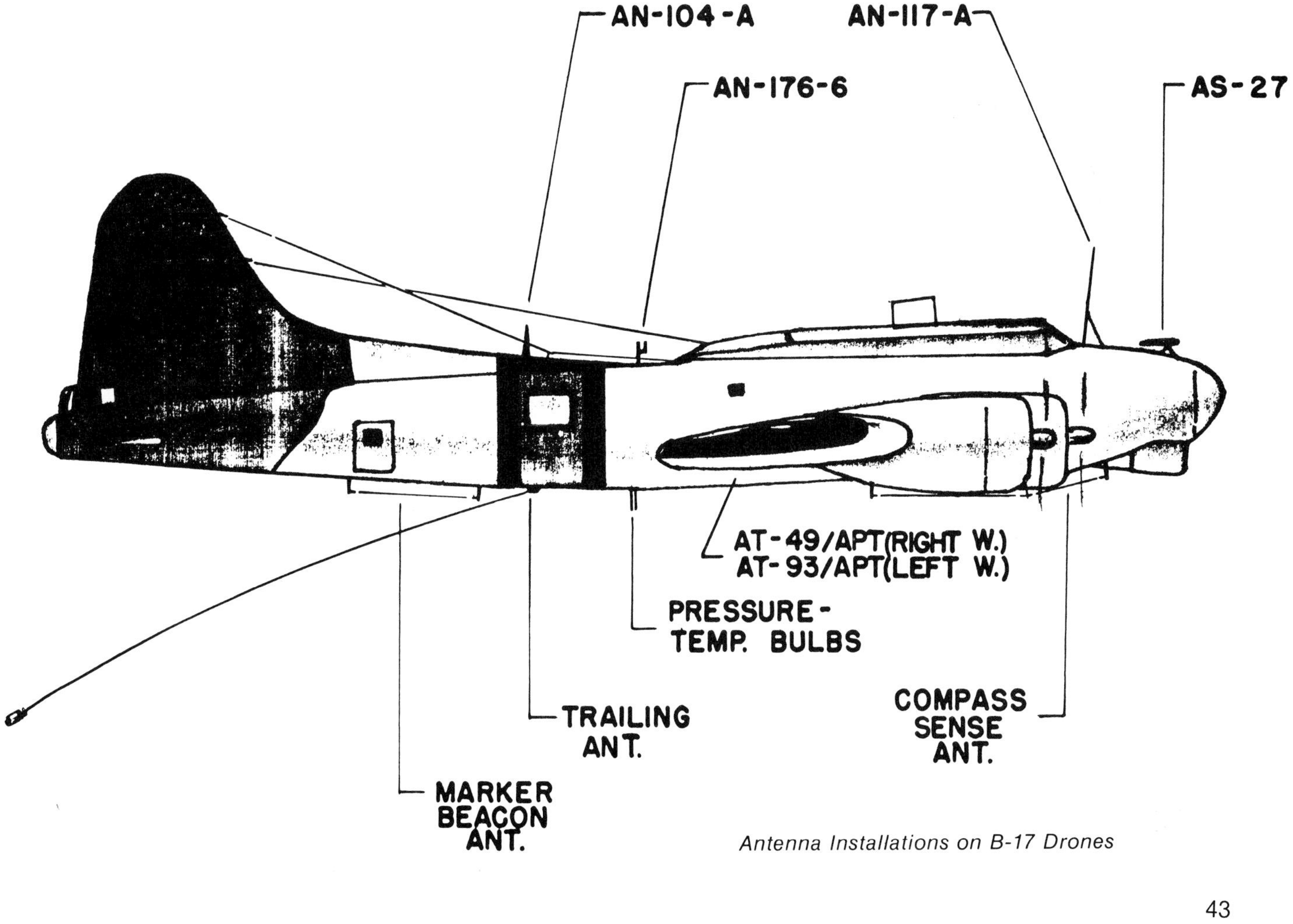

Antenna Installations on B-17 Drones

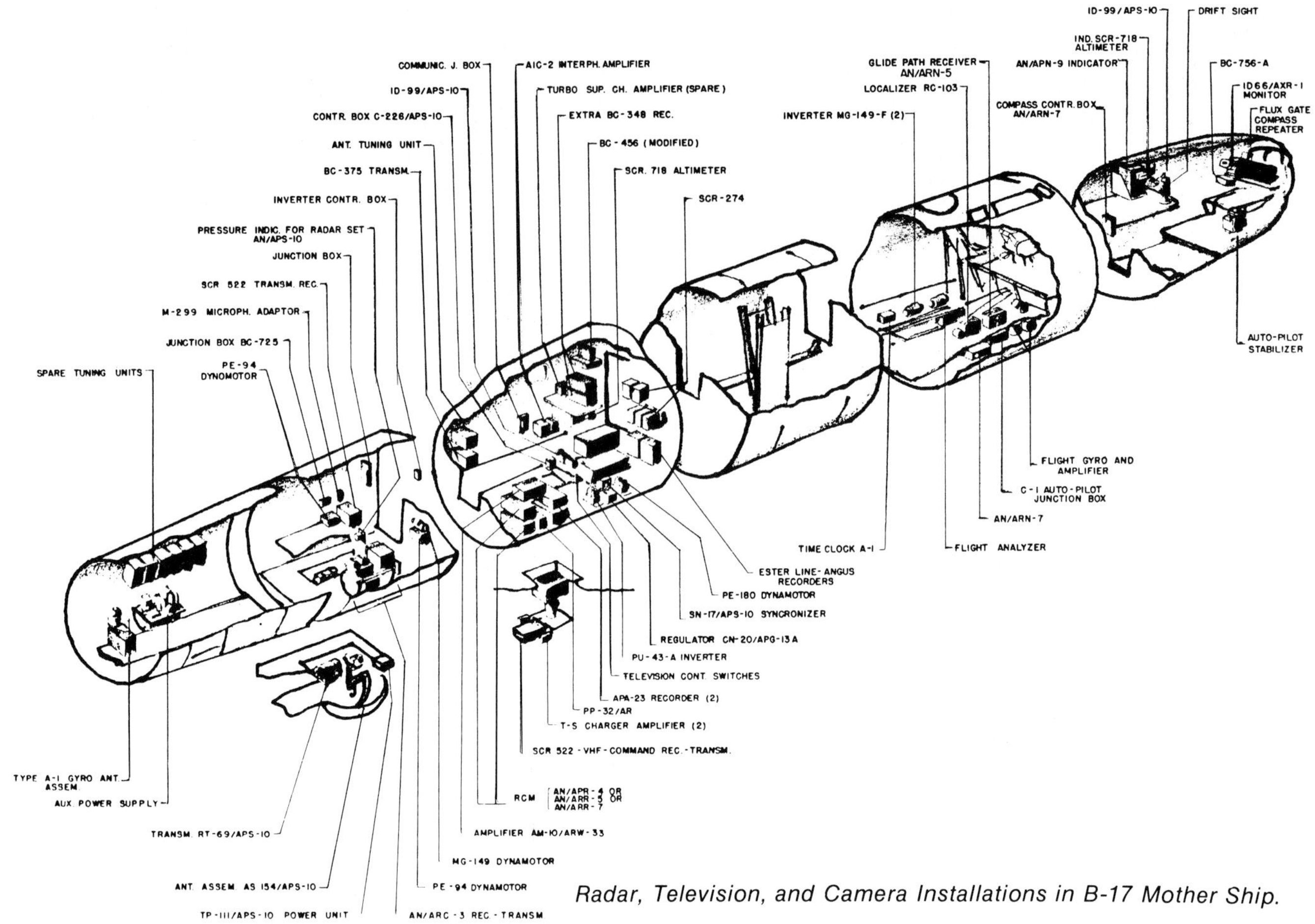

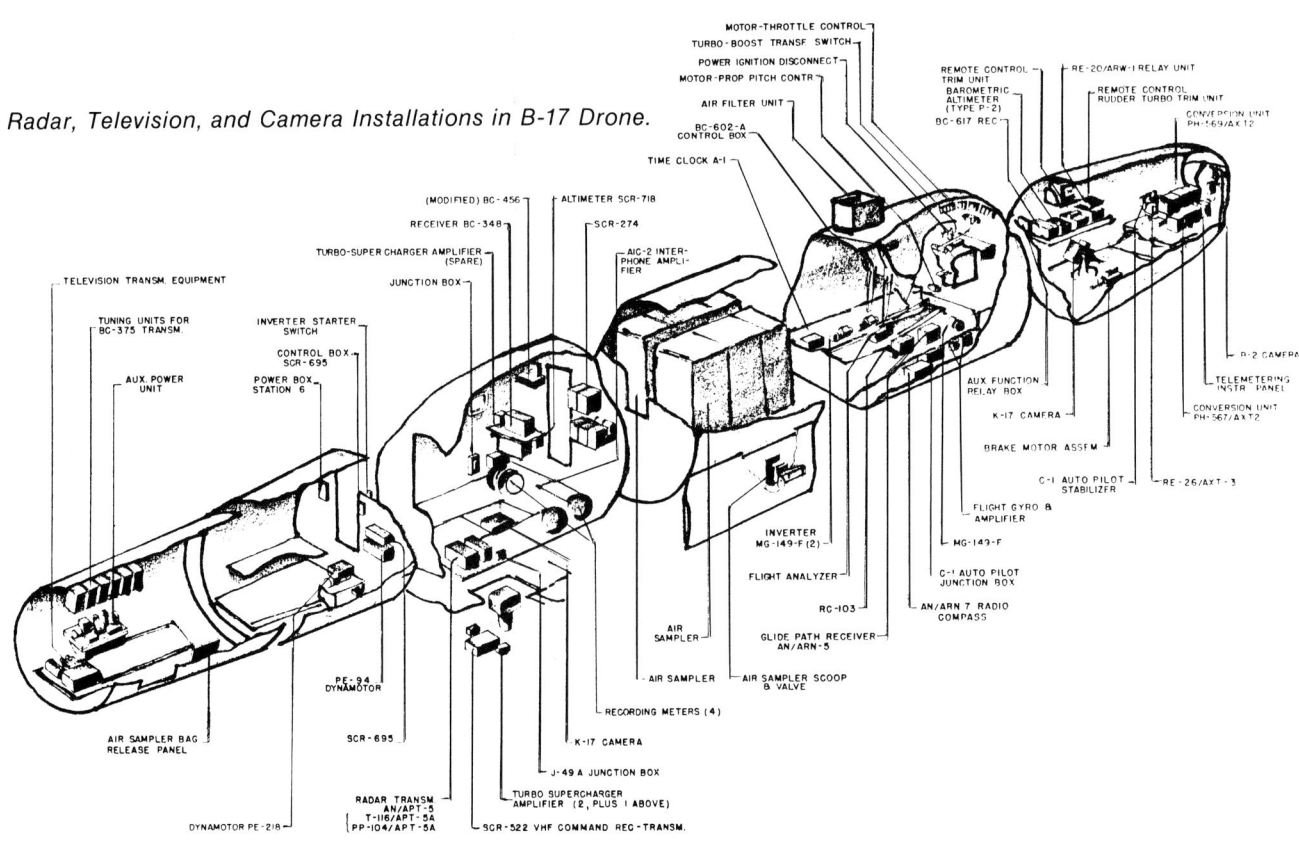

Radar, Television, and Camera Installations in B-17 Mother Ship.

Radar, Television, and Camera Installations in B-17 Drone.

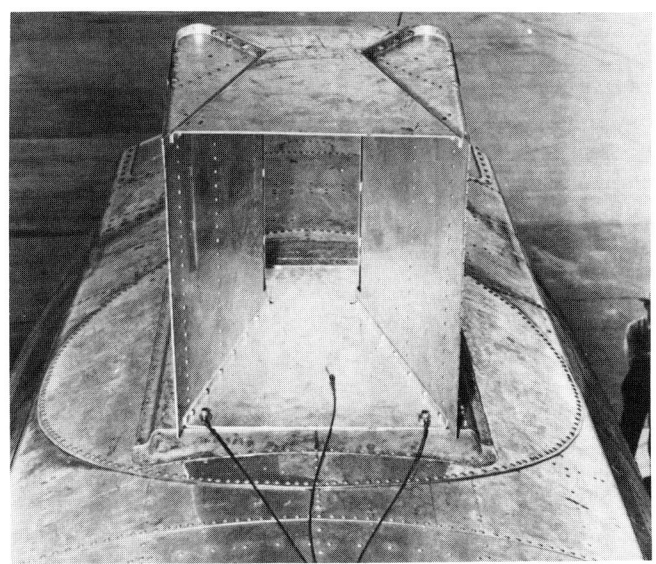

An air filter unit was installed in the top turret location on drone aircraft number 2, s/n 44-83553. Air captured in this device was directed to air sampler bags located in the bomb bay. (USAF)

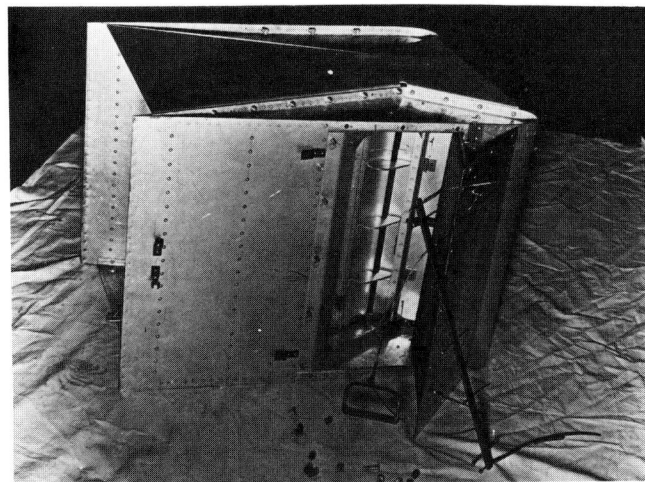

This side view of the "bug catcher" used on the QB-17 shows the filter assembly compartment. (USAF)

A pair of these air sampler bags would be installed in the bomb bays of the drone aircraft. (USAF)

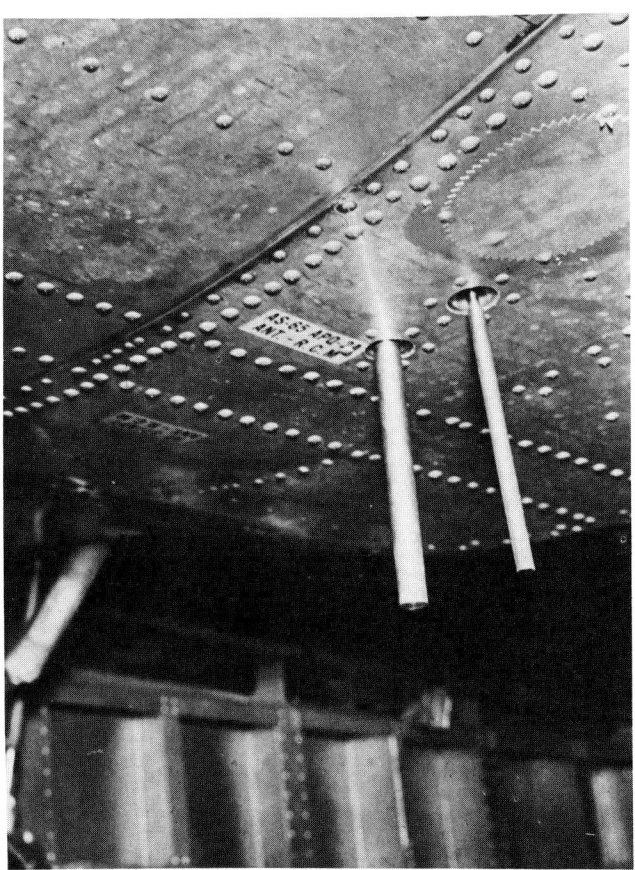

A pair of free air bulbs was installed aft of the bomb bay on the drone ships. (USAF)

Supports were added to the bomb bay to hold the air bag. (USAF)

External view of the B-2 Jerome camera installation in a drone ship. (USAF)

Interior view of the B-2 Jerome camera and television installation in a drone ship. (USAF)

The instrument panel of a drone aircraft showing its set-up switches and throttle control linkages. (USAF)

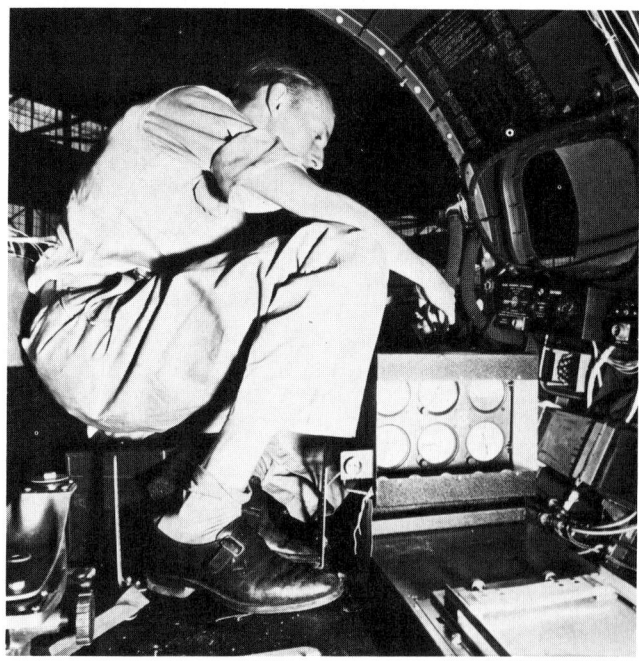

The telemetry instruments were carried in the right side of the nose on the drone aircraft. (USAF)

An AN/APR-4 radio countermeasures receiver was installed in the aft left section of the radio compartment of the drone control ships. (USAF)

The K-17 camera is shown being installed in the radio compartment. (USAF)

This view is looking aft into the nose section of a drone ship. Included in the equipment was a C-1 autopilot stabilizer, remote control trim unit, P-2 barometric altimeter, and provisions for a K-17 vertically mounted camera. (USAF)

This AN/APT-5 jamming transmitter was installed on one of the drones to test effectiveness during the blast. This unit was located in the aft section of the radio compartment. (USAF)

Interior view of the ID66/AXR-1 television monitor and the drone control box. (USAF)

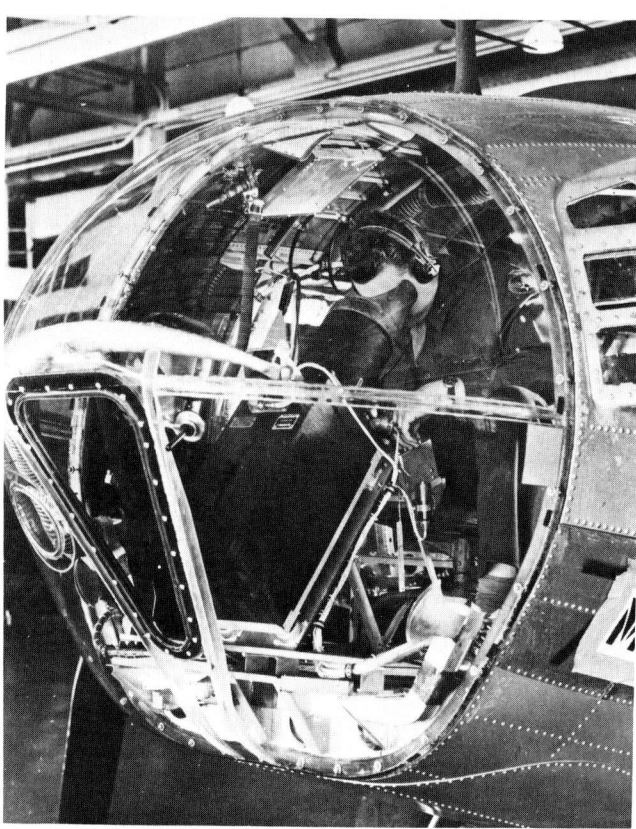
External view of an ID66/AXR-1 television monitor and control box in a drone control ship. (USAF)

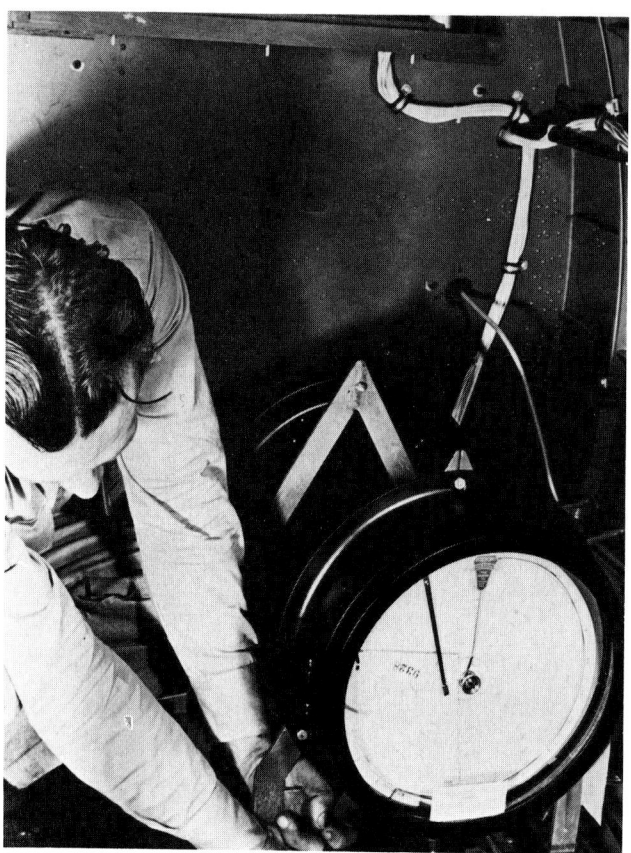
Four of these Foxboro pressure recorders were carried in the radio compartment of the drone ships. (USAF)

This Hathaway flight analyzer was installed beneath the cockpit floor just aft of the pilot's seat. (USAF)

QB-17 DRONES

A QB-17L is prepared for dispatch. The aircraft was painted overall day-glo orange with black lettering.(Boeing 138362)

A number of B-17s were converted for drone operations so as to provide aerial platform applications which would be too hazardous for crews of manned aircraft. In the early-to-mid 1940s the designator BQ-7 was allocated to this B-17 version. After 1947 the designation QB-17 was used. The two aircraft in this category were the QB-17L and QB-17N, whose differences follow:

QB-17L - A target drone conversion of the B-17G having TV cameras in addition to remote control equipment.

QB-17N - Similar to the QB-17L but with additional radio control equipment and the TV transmitters deleted.

See the following Main Differences Table comparing the B-17G, QB-17L and QB-17N:

Airframe Changes

A number of changes were made to the airframe group compartments on the basic B-17 in order to accommodate the mission equipment peculiar to the QB-17. Some of these changes include installation of modified wingtips for the camera stores, modification of the wing flap indicating system to provide visual indication of the flap position at night, modification to the surface control system to accommodate the automatic pilot system, and relocation of the fuselage bomb bay door electrical control switch and indicator lights.

The fuselage compartments were reestablished in order to accommodate the mission equipment. These changes are shown on the figure at the top of page 52.

MAIN DIFFERENCES TABLE

DIFFERENCES	B-17G	QB-17L	QB-17N
CREW	TEN	FOUR (ON TRAINING FLIGHTS)	FOUR (ON TRAINING FLIGHTS)
ARMAMENT	ALL	NONE	NONE
CAMERA SCORING SYSTEM	NONE	SOME	SOME
DE-ICING SYSTEM	ALL	NONE	NONE
INVERTERS	TWO	FOUR	FOUR
EXTERNAL POWER RECEPTACLES	ONE	TWO	TWO
AUTOPILOT	TYPE C-1	TYPE E-4	TYPE E-4
NIGHT MISSION LIGHTING	NONE	ALL	ALL
GUIDANCE EQUIPMENT	NONE	AN/ARW-40 AND AN/ARW-1C	AN/ARW-64
TELEVISION EQUIPMENT	NONE	AN/AXT-3B WITH PH-563/AXT	NONE
TELEMETERING EQUIPMENT	NONE	NONE	AN/AKT-7
RANGE SAFETY	NONE	AN/URW-2	PART OF AN/ARW-64

This QB-17L was used for testing the Boeing IM-99 Bomarc interceptor missile. The night mission lighting installation was located in the nose. The aircraft was painted overall day-glo orange, and had three thirty-six inch wide diagonal belly stripes. This picture was taken at Cape Canaveral, Florida, on January 30, 1956.   (USAF 158901 AC/Boeing HS-907)

Landing Gear System

The basic B-17 landing gear system was altered by modification of the gear extension and retraction controls, modification of the main gear brake system, the addition of an external release for the tail wheel lock, and the addition of an arresting hook on the tail wheel scissor link assembly.

DSCSE

The major airplane modification was the installation of the drone stabilization control system (DSCSE). Instruments were added to the pilot's instrument panel to include an auxiliary instrument panel which was added to the QB-17L for the TV system. The automatic pilot system was changed to replace the Type C-1 system with an E-4 system, and autopilot control units were added. The DSCSE provided flight path stabilization through signals transmitted from the ground or airborne radio stations. The following controls were operated by the DSCSE:

- Aileron control
- Rudder control
- Elevator control
- Elevator trim tab control
- Flap extension and retraction
- Landing gear retraction and extension
- Brake application
- Throttle control
- Mixture control
- Propeller pitch control
- Turbosupercharger control
- Fuel tank (Tokyo) shutoff valve control
- Auxiliary power plant control
- Camera scoring system
- Range safety system

Electrical System

A number of electrical system changes were necessitated by the additional mission equipment. The four major components consisted of:

- Special inverter box
- Special external power receptacle
- Auxiliary junction box
- Special inverter PU-16

Radio and Radar Systems

A number of changes were made to the radio and radar systems in order to permit the aircraft to operate in the drone role. A summary of the equipment installations follows:

AN/ARC-27	UHF Command Radio
AN/ARC-3	VHF Radio Set
AN/AXT-3B	Radio Transmitting System (QB-17L)
DY-25/AXT-2	Dynamotor (QB-17L)
AN/ART-7	Telemetering Transmitting Set (QB-17N)
AN/ARW-40	Radio Receiving Set (QB-17L)
AN/ARW-1C	Radio Receiving Set (QB-17N)
AN/URW-2	Range Safety System (QB-17L)
BC-453	Radio Range Receiver

The scoring camera exposure data and film combinations were as follows:

Camera	Frame Rate (FPS)	Exposure	Film
16mm Filmo	200	1/1000	Eastman Daylight Kodachrome
16mm Fastax	500	1/2500	Standard pitch (0.3000 inch) special packed Eastman Daylight Kodachrome
16mm Triad-200	200	1/1000	Eastman Daylight Kodachrome with Wrattan 2-B filter
35mm Ultra-Speed	200	1/1000	Ansco color negative

QB-17N, s/n 43-39340, with the wingtip camera scoring system installed. This aircraft was painted overall day-glo red with a silver rudder. The upper wing surfaces were white. (W.J. Balough via G.S. Williams)

Camera Scoring System

A Douglas Aircraft-designed camera scoring system was made for the QB-17Ls and -Ns. This system was carried in wingtip-mounted pods. Without the pods all dimensions for the aircraft were identical to those on the B-17G. The existing aircraft wingtips could be removed for installation of camera pods. The revised wingtips were contoured for installation of the pods. With the camera pods installed, the wing span was reduced from 103' 9.38" to 102'. The drawing on page 54 shows the dimensional differences.

The scoring camera stores were droppable aluminum pods. The major components in each pod were three 16mm cameras, one 35mm camera, a battery, a dynamotor, and two heater and blower units. In the event of an emergency release, the stores were equipped with a parachute recovery system and flotation bags installed in the removable tip of the aft section of the pod. A fifty-four inch drogue parabrake was installed in the aft section of the tail cone, while a forty foot diameter main parachute was located in the forward position of the tail cone.

The optical scoring camera system was designed to provide a record of the passage in space of a missile with respect to its target (the QB-17). The photographic evidence was used for photogrametric missile miss vector determination in order to determine the shooter's score.

The scoring cameras were arranged so as to provide complete photographic coverage of the entire spherical field of view about the QB-17. Each camera was provided with a means of recording a common time base. The system consisted of four cameras located in each of the two camera stores.

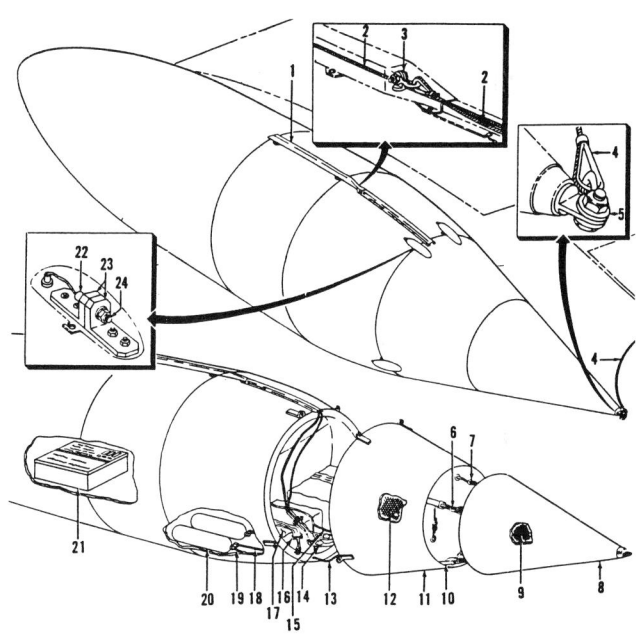

Scoring Camera Stores Recovery Equipment

1 SUSPENSION CABLES FAIRING
2 MAIN PARACHUTE SUSPENSION CABLE
3 STORE LOAD FITTING
4 STATIC LINE
5 CONE STATIC LINE ATTACHMENT
6 PARABRAKE SUSPENSION LINE
7 MAIN PARACHUTE DEPLOYMENT BAG ATTACHMENT
8 AFT CONE ASSEMBLY
9 PARABRAKE
10 PARABRAKE-CONE ATTACHMENT
11 FORWARD CONE ASSEMBLY
12 MAIN PARACHUTE
13 DISCHARGE PULL CORD
14 MAIN PARACHUTE HARNESS
15 FLOTATION BAG PULL CORD
16 LIFT WEB ASSEMBLY
17 FLOTATION BAG
18 DISCHARGE HOSE
19 DISCHARGE CABLE
20 CO_2 BOTTLE
21 PARACHUTE RECOVERY CONTROL BOX
22 EXPLOSIVE BOLT DETONATOR
23 CONE ATTACHMENT FITTING
24 CONE EXPLOSIVE BOLT

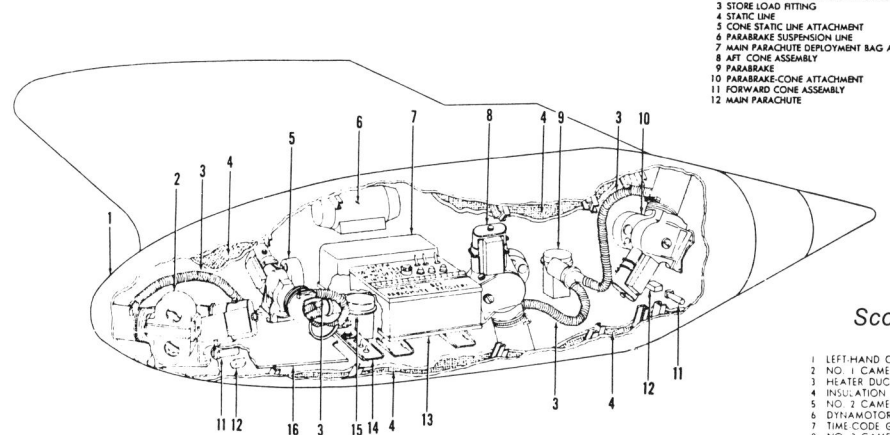

Scoring Camera Store (Left Hand)

1 LEFT-HAND CAMERA STORE
2 NO. 1 CAMERA
3 HEATER DUCT
4 INSULATION
5 NO. 2 CAMERA
6 DYNAMOTOR
7 TIME CODE GENERATOR
8 NO. 3 CAMERA
9 AFT HEATER
10 NO. 4 CAMERA
11 THERMO SWITCH
12 CONDENSER
13 PARACHUTE RECOVERY CONTROL BOX
14 SWITCH PANEL
15 FORWARD HEATER
16 FLOOR

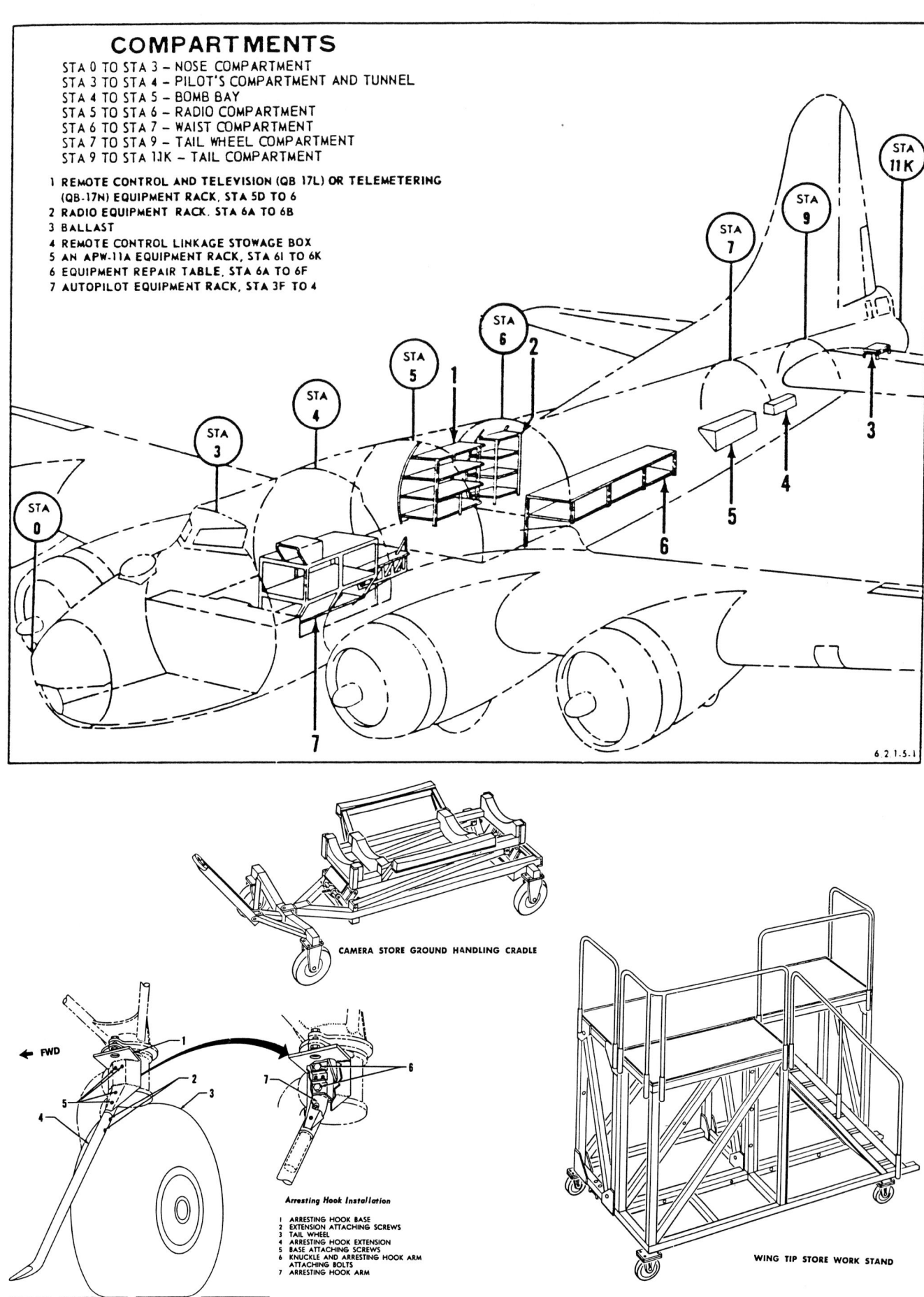

antenna locations

1. STATIC DISCHARGERS
2. GUIDANCE RADIO ANTENNA
3. TELEVISION ANTENNA
4. RANGE RECEIVER ANTENNA
5. VHF RADIO ANTENNA
6. RADAR ANTENNAS
7. LIAISON RADIO ANTENNA
8. RANGE SAFETY RADIO ANTENNA
9. MARKER BEACON ANTENNA
10. LIAISON RADIO TRAILING ANTENNA
11. UHF RADIO ANTENNA
12. RADIO COMPASS LOOP ANTENNA
13. RADIO COMPASS SENSE ANTENNA
14. ILS ANTENNA

External Lighting System

The external lighting system was enhanced to include wing flood lights, landing gear lights, night mission lights, and, on the QB-17L, fuel transfer lights.

QB-17N, s/n 44-83669, was at Patrick AFB, Florida, in 1954. The aircraft was overall day-glo orange with three thirty-six inch black diagonal stripes. (G.S. Williams)

Right front quarter view of QB-17N, s/n 44-83669. (G.S. Williams)

TABLE III
EXTERIOR LIGHTING SYSTEM COMPONENT LOCATION

COMPONENT	TYPE	LOCATION
Wing Floodlights		
Right Wing Light	General Electric No. 4570	At station 5C on the right side of the radio room.
Left Wing Light	General Electric No. 4570	At station 5C on the left side of the radio room.
Landing Gear Lights		
Right Landing Gear Light.	General Electric No. 4570	Inside right wheel well.
Left Landing Gear Light.	General Electric No. 4570	Inside left wheel well.
Flap Indicating Lights		
Right Flap Light.	AN3030-5	At the approximate center of the right wing flap.
Left Flap Light.	AN3030-5	At the approximate center of the left wing flap.
Exterior Mission Lights		
Dorsal Fin Light	AN3097-2	At station 9A at the top of the dorsal fin.
Left Tail Cone Lights	AN3033-7	Top left side of the tail cone at station 11E.
	AN3033-7	Bottom left side of the tail cone at station 11E.
Right Tail Cone Lights	AN3033-8	Top right side of the tail cone at station 11E.
	AN3033-8	Bottom right side of the tail cone at station 11E.
Front Mission Lights	AN3033-8	Right side of the nose at station 2C.
	AN3033-7	Left side of the nose at station 2C.
Fuel Transfer Lights (QB-17L)		
Right Fuel Transfer Light	AN3158-2	Right side of the tail cone just below center.
Left Fuel Transfer Light	AN3158-2	Left side of the tail cone just below center.

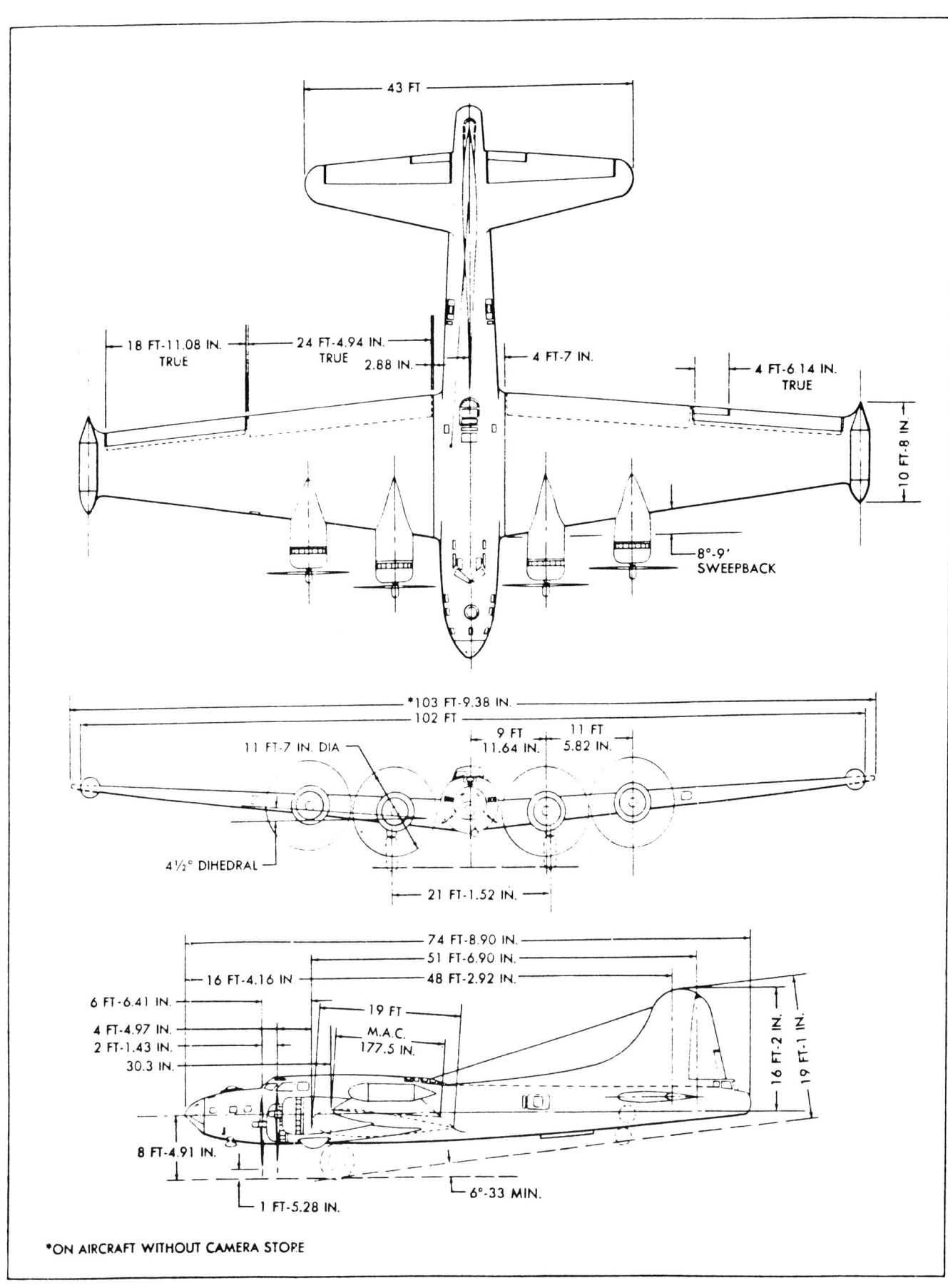

Right front quarter view of QB-17N, s/n 43-39340, reveals some of the white upper wing surfaces. Black anti-glare paint was applied to the upper inboard quadrant of the nacelles and cowls, and to the nose. (G.S. Williams)

QB-17N, s/n 44-83555, at Holloman AFB, New Mexico, on November 16, 1956. (USAF)

Left rear quarter view of QB-17N, s/n 44-83555, reveals the additional radio compartment window for the wing floodlights. (USAF)

QB-17L, 44-85662, was overall day-glo orange with thirty-six inch black stripes. The rudder was silver, while the tail insignia was red, white, and blue. (D.W. Menard)

DB-17 DRONE DIRECTOR

DB-17P-90-DL, s/n 44-83684, carried the insignia for the USAF Air Defense Weapons Center on the fin. (For the modeler, this insignia is available on Microscale Sheet 72-198.) (W.J. Balough via G.S. Williams)

Several B-17s were converted for the drone director role. Initially these aircraft were designated as CQ-4s. By 1948 this designation had been changed to DB-17P. These aircraft continued in service until 1960.

This same aircraft is seen with the number 3 and 4 engines turning. The guidance radio whip antenna is visible on top of the fuselage. This aircraft was photographed at Eglin AFB, Florida, in 1956. (W.J. Balough via G.S. Williams)

WINGTIP GUNNER'S STATION

B-17G-95-DL, 44-85784 reveals its buzz number and the aft end of the gunner's station. (P.M. Bowers B.3330)

In 1949, B-17G-95-DL, 44-85784, was modified to accept a manned wingtip pod. This position was to be manned by a gunner. Although the wing of the B-17 was relatively stiff, the wingtip oscillations were unbearable resulting in a high degree of air sickness. Needless to say, the project was abandoned. The aircraft carried a buzz number aft of the national insignia on the fuselage. It was located above the crew door on the right side of the fuselage and extended forward above the bar, stopping at the circle on the national insignia.

B-17G-95-DL, 44-85784, shown parked in front of Hangar No. 1, Area D, Wright Field on May 3, 1949. The wingtip pod is visible near the tail of B-17G-95-VE, 44-85570. (NASM 84-11153)

This close-up view of the wingtip pod shows the clear nose piece. A tiedown rope may be seen hanging from the outboard wing panel. (NASM 84-11152)

WEATHER RECON B-17s

B-17G-90-BO, 43-38522 of the 53rd Reconnaissance Squadron, Long Range (Weather) during the 1944-1945 time period. The 53rd RS operated these aircraft from Presque Isle AAFld, Maine, between August 31, 1944, and November 9, 1944; Grenier Field, New Hampshire, between November 9, 1944, and November 8, 1946; and Morrison Field, Florida, between November 8, 1946, and July 21, 1947.

(USAF)

During World War II, the USAF operated armed B-17s for weather reconnaissance out of England. The 652nd RS of the 25th RG (Weather) operated these aircraft out of Watton, Alconbury, and Raydon, England. Initially the weather reconnaissance mission was flown with a B-17 without any specialized equipment. Then the RAF supplied weather specialists and equipment for the aircraft, and later the USAAF provided its own technicians. These aircraft would fly at fifty mile intervals west bound from England at altitudes of fifty and five hundred feet for 1,000 miles, then they would stair step in five hundred foot increments to 30,000 feet. They would broadcast their findings in code interspersed with Radio America and ball game scores. The aircraft would then head for the Azores to permit a crew rest period. The return trip was flown to a point in the Atlantic 1,500 miles west of England, and the flight plan was flown in reverse ending at 30,000 feet above England.

A similar operation was flown by the 53rd RS out of Presque Isle AAFld, Maine, and Grenier Field, New Hampshire, in order to provide coverage of the western Atlantic.

Later, a number of B-17s were modified specifically for the weather reconnaissance role. In January 1945 one F-9 and three B-17Fs were converted for use by the 3rd RS. The following modifications were made:

Removals
- All photographic equipment
- All turrets, guns, armor plate, bombsight, bomb hoists and bomb shackles

Installations
- SCR-269 or AN/ARN-7 radio compass with one indicator and control box in the pilot's compartment, and one indicator and control box in the navigator's compartment
- RC-103A and AN/ARN-5 blind landing system
- RC-193 marker beacon, complete with indicator light and antennas
- AN/APN-4 or AN/APN-9 LORAN with controls and indicator in the navigator's compartment
- SCR-274 command set with BC-453A, BC-454, BC-455, BC-457 and BC-458 components, and BC-459.
- SCR-522 VHF radio with the controls in the cockpit
- SCR-718A radio altimeter with its indicator and controls in the navigator's compartment
- AN/APN-1 low altitude radio altimeter with ID-14/APN-1 indicator, altitude limit indicator lights, and altitude limit switch in the cockpit
- AN/ART-13 radio complete with low frequency components, and operator's spare part kit in the radio compartment
- Two BC-348 radio receivers in the radio compartment
- Very (flare) pistol and cartridges
- B-3 driftmeter in the navigator's compartment
- Gyro fluxgate compass with the master indicator located in the navigator's compartment and remote indicator located in the cockpit
- Supercharger electronic control system
- ML-313/AM aircraft psychrometer in the navigator's compartment
- AN/AMQ-3 aerograph in the navigator's compartment

In addition, the aircraft were winterized.

These modifications were accomplished at Buckley Field, Colorado, by the Air Technical Service Command.

In April 1945, nine production B-17s were converted for weather reconnaissance. These aircraft were converted by the Air Technical Service Command. These modifications included:

- Two 410 gallon bomb bay fuel tanks
- A second pressure altimeter on the weather observer's instrument panel
- A table with a plexiglass top for the weather

observer. The table was twenty inches deep and thirty-six inches long, curved to fit the contour of the fuselage and mounted on the left side above the weather observer's instrument panel. This installation permitted visibility on the instruments mounted on the panel.
- A second navigator's seat for use by the weather observer
- In connection with the AN/APN-1 low altitude radio altimeter, a second indicator was mounted above the SCR-718 radio altimeter indicator in the weather observer's compartment
- Provisions for an additional inverter were made in case the electrical loads from the LORAN equipment exceeded the capability of the original single inverter
- Windshield wipers for the pilot's and copilot's windows
- An A-11 clock in the radio compartment
- A Stewart-Warner cockpit heater (50,000 BTU)
- A C-13 bimetalic thermometer to indicate cabin temperature on the instrument panel in the weather observer's compartment
- Outboard wing "Tokyo" tanks

The 30th RS operated up to twenty-one B-17s in the weather reconnaissance role. They had detachments at McChord Field, Washington; Gander Lake, Newfoundland; and Grenier Field, Manchester, New Hampshire.

B-17G-95-BO, 43-38785, was also flown by the 53rd WRS. The chin turret had been removed and the turret hole faired over. The psychrometer may be seen just above the pitot probe. An RC-103 Glide Slope antenna was mounted on the top of the nose. (USAF)

TB-17G-85-DL, 44-83571, with nineteen weather bird mission markers. This photo was taken at Boeing Field. (G.S. Williams)

Close-up of the nose marking on B-17G-35-VE, 42-97908, flown by the 53rd WRS. (USAF)

This ground crew is servicing a 53rd RS TB-17G weather ship.

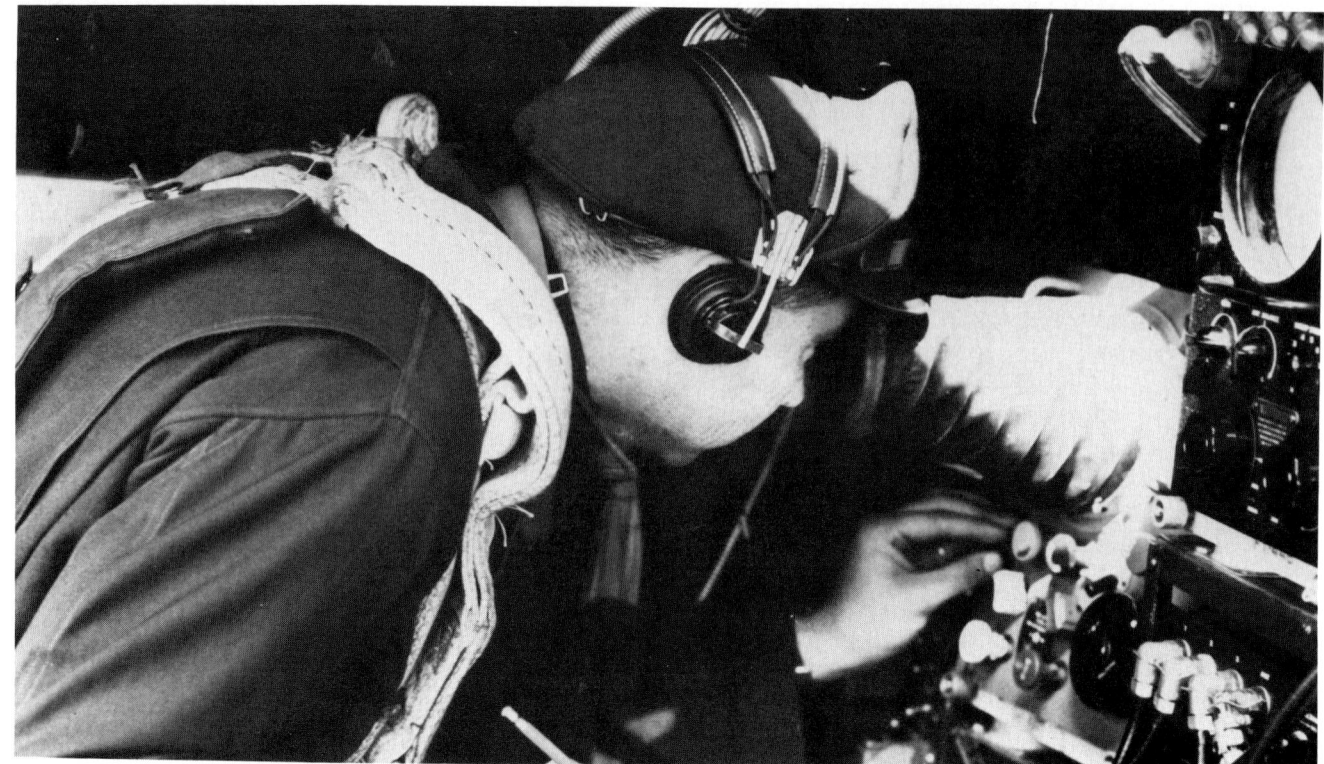

A 652nd WRS, 25th RG (Weather) navigator operating a "Gee" Box (radar) on a B-17. The unit operated out of England during World War II. This photo was dated May 23, 1945. (USAF)

Left: A 652nd WRS, 25th RG (Weather) technician drops a flare through a port in the waist of a B-17 weather ship in order to determine the drift. This photo was dated May 25, 1945. (USAF)

Below right: An exterior view of the psychrometer installation on a weather B-17. (USAF)

Below left: An interior view of the psychrometer installation on a weather B-17. (USAF)

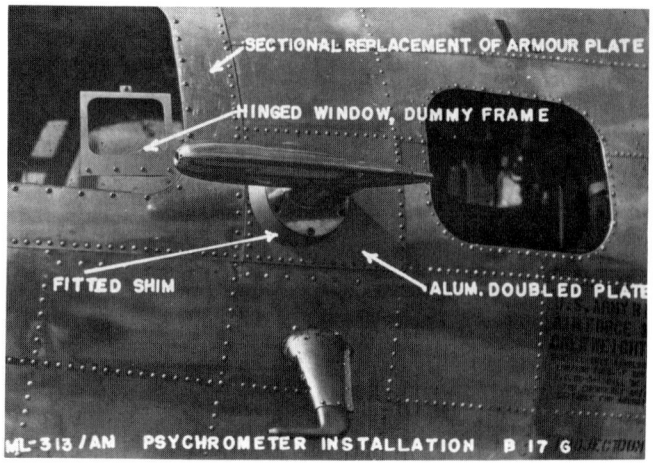

ALL WEATHER FLYING CENTER

TB-17G-70-VE, 44-8543 at Patterson Field. (P.M. Bowers)

The All Weather Flying Center operated a variety of aircraft out of Clinton County Army Airfield, Ohio, between March 9, 1946, and October 16, 1949. From there they moved to Wright-Patterson AFB, Ohio. Their mission was to develop equipment and procedures for all weather flying. One aircraft was tasked to fly daily between Ohio and Andrews AFB in Maryland, regardless of the weather.

The aircraft had red vertical tails, engine cowls, and noses. A yellow line was applied to the aft edge of the nose color.

Some aircraft types operated by the AWFC included B-17s, C-54s, B-29s, C-82s.

Right front quarter view of the same aircraft as seen above. (P.M. Bowers)

This view of another AWFC TB-17G reveals a buzz number reading BA-837 beneath the left outboard wing panel. The No. 2 engine cowling was painted yellow, and **ALL WEATHER FLYING CENTER** was applied beneath the cockpit. (P.M. Bowers)

CLOUD PHYSICS PROJECT

Right front view of one of the Cloud Physics Project's B-17s. (USAF via M. Rodina)

During the 1950s, at least three TB-17Gs were modified for use in the Cloud Physics Project, and were known to have operated out of Olmstead AFB, Pennsylvania. All armament was removed, and in lieu of the top turret, a project director's station was installed. The nose was extensively revised to include a variety of sensors and a radar antenna. The aircraft would fly into cloud areas, and at the direction of the project director, would perform cloud seeding tests. Two of the aircraft were B-17G-80-DL, s/n 44-83461, and B-17G-90-DL, s/n 44-83587.

*B-17G-90-DL, s/n 44-83587, with the name **Nancy** beneath the tail insignia. The tail marking appears to be a blue disc, white cloud, and red lightning bolt.* (USAF via M. Rodina)

*The name **CLOUD PHYSICS PROJECT** was applied to both the left and right sides of the nose on this aircraft.*
(USAF via M. Rodina)

This close-up of the right side of the nose reveals many of the sensors.
(USAF via M. Rodina)

This assortment of sensors was mounted on TB-17G-80-DL, s/n 44-83461.
(USAF via M. Rodina)

In this front view the chin turret plug is revealed. A number of the sensors had openings in their forward surfaces for sample collection. No less than twelve sensors (in addition to the standard pitot probe) may be seen around the circumference of the nose.
(USAF via M. Rodina)

Above left: This close-up reveals the project director's dome and a new data block beneath the pilot's window.
(USAF via M. Rodina)

Above right: A standard wooden office chair with shoulder harness appears within the project director's dome.
(USAF via M. Rodina)

Equipment racks in the left waist position of the aircraft.
(USAF via M. Rodina)

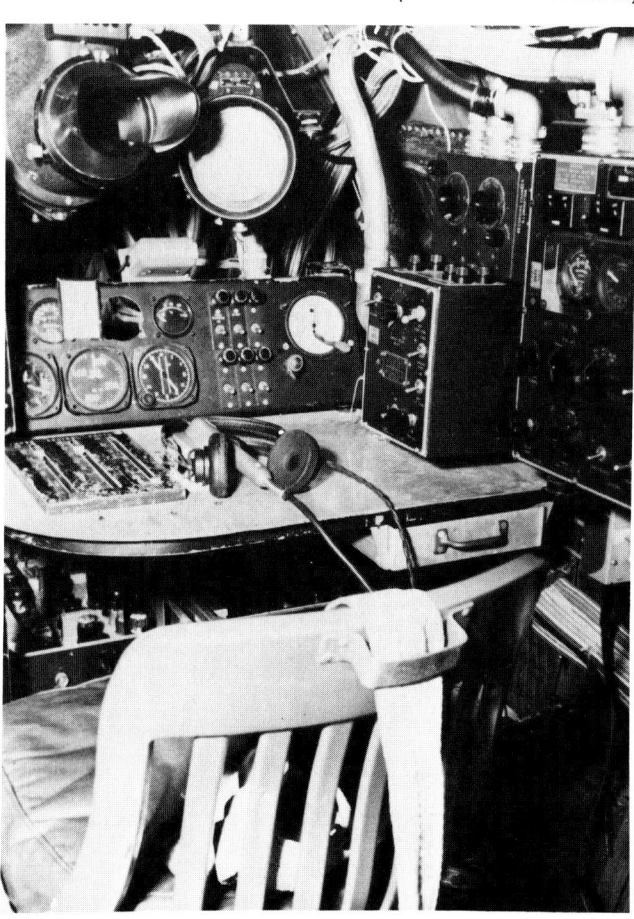

The weather technician's station was located in the radio compartment, and included radar scopes.
(USAF via M. Rodina)

Left: Front view of the radar antenna and the nose fairing required for the radome are apparent in this picture.
(USAF via M. Rodina)

ETB-17

This oblique view reveals both the upper and lower ADF loop antennas. Being a late-model B-17, the inboard exhaust duct is shrouded. The inboard surface of the wingtip antennas were flat. (O'Dell via G.S. Williams)

During the mid-1950s ETB-17G-70-VE, s/n 44-8543, was bailed to the Federal Telecommunications Corporation in Teterboro, New Jersey. This aircraft was stripped of all armament, and a second ADF loop antenna was installed in the faired over top turret location. Large box-like antennas were fitted to the wingtips.

This right rear view reveals the curvature to the top surface of the wingtip antenna. The 0- before the tail number indicated that the aircraft was over ten years old.
(O'Dell via G.S. Williams)

Six flat surfaces made up the outboard edge of the wingtip antenna. (NASM 77-11568)

The surface details on the wingtip antenna are clearly visible in this view. (O'Dell via G.S. Williams)

CIVILIAN MODIFICATIONS

B-17G-95-VE, 44-85507, became N5116N. It served as Colonel Robert McCormick's personal aircraft at the Chicago Tribune before going to Hurd Mapping, Co. as depicted here on August 15, 1952. She carries a tail cone similar to General MacArthur's C-108. The flags adjacent to the aft entry door are representative of her travels. A heater inlet was added to the stabilizer.
(W.T. Larkins via G.S. Williams)

B-17G-95-DL, 44-83735, carried a "Limited" certificate and was registered as NL68269. The aircraft was named **San Miguel,** and was owned by the president of Philippine Airlines. This photo dates from 1947.
(C. Johnson via G.S. Williams)

B-17G-95-DL, 44-83872, became PB-1W, BuNo 77235, before carrying civil registry N7227C. The aircraft performed aerial survey work for the Aero Service Corporation based in Philadelphia, Pennsylvania. The aircraft was photographed while leaving Boeing Field, Seattle, Washington.
(Boeing P39448)

Another Aero Service ship was N3193G, ex-B-17G-110-VE, 44-85826, and PB-1G, BuNo 77255.
(G.S. Williams)

B-17 SPRAYER

TB-17F-70-BO, 42-29782, became N17W operated by Central Aircraft of Yakima, Washington, after serving as a monument in Springfield, Missouri. This aircraft flew in the movie "Tora, Tora, Tora", and now resides in Seattle, Washington, as a potential acquisition for the Museum of Flight. (via G.S. Williams)

N17W was equipped with a pair of tanks capable of carrying 15,000 pounds of insecticide. A spray bar was mounted from the aft edge of the bomb bay. (via G.S. Williams)

This view of N17W reveals the spray bars and tanks. (via G.S. Williams)

N17W also carried spray bars under the wings. (via G.S. Williams)

N17W, shown with a new paint job at Biegert Brothers, was photographed in Phoenix, Arizona. (via G.S. Williams)

MODEL 299AB

Left front quarter view of the Model 299AB on the east side of Boeing Field on August 9, 1947. (Boeing 97287B)

The Boeing Model 299AB was an executive conversion of B-17G-105-VE, s/n 44-85728. This aircraft was purchased from the U.S. Government in 1946 by TWA and ferried to Boeing-Seattle for conversion. The first civil registration applied to the aircraft was NX4600, the X being for experimental. Subsequently, the registration was changed to NL-1B when the aircraft was issued a limited type certificate, because it could not qualify for a standard commercial license (NC). This aircraft was used by TWA to survey post war routes in the Near East. In late 1947, TWA gave the aircraft to the Shah of Iran. The aircraft was then registered as EP-HIM, for "His Imperial Majesty".

Right front quarter view of the Model 299AB. (Boeing 97290B)

Right rear view of the Model 299AB showing the extra waist windows and the faired over waist gun window.
(Boeing 2789B)

Above: A flight engineer's seat was installed between the pilots on Model 299AB. (Boeing A24506)

The Model 299AB is seen here after transfer to the Shah of Iran with the new registration, EP-HIM. (via G.S. Williams)

The Shah's crest appeared on the fin, nose, and wing. (via G.S. Williams)

The modified tail position on the Model 299AB. (Boeing 27286B)

RESTORED B-17s

The famed 91st BG ship **Memphis Belle**, B-17F-10-BO, 42-24485, DF-A, resides as a memorial in Memphis, Tennessee. During restoration, the airplane received a B-17G top turret and fictitious codes, MJ5, on the waist. This picture was taken in 1965.
(G.S. Williams)

The **Sentimental Journey** is a B-17G which is almost fully restored, and is owned and operated by the Arizona Wing of the Confederate Air Force. It is shown here flying over the Seattle area for the B-17 Fiftieth Anniversary celebrations.
(Boeing JBB179)

This B-17G is owned and operated by Dave Tallichet. Although it is a B-17G, it is painted to resemble a B-17F from the 100th BG.
(Boeing JJB170)

Memories lived on as **Sentimental Journey** and Dave Tallichet's aircraft flew with their "Little Friends" during the B-17 Fiftieth Anniversary celebration in Seattle, Washington, on July 26, 1985.
(Boeing)

One of the restored B-17Gs owned by the Royal Air Force Museum is shown in flight. It is restored to represent a Flying Fortress from the 508th BS of the 351st BG, 1st AD, 8th AF.
(Pealing via Jury)

MODELER'S SECTION

Since this book deals with derivatives of the B-17, no standard kits are available for review. Therefore, we are departing from our usual format for the "Modeler's Section", and are explaining the basics of how to do a conversion for some of the derivatives covered in this volume. For the most part, these conversions are more difficult than building a stock kit, and are recommended for the more experienced modeler. In all cases, extensive research should be done on the specific aircraft being modeled. These conversions require a varying degree of effort, time, and patience, but should provide some interesting model building. The resulting model will be rewarding, and should be one not seen on just any modeler's display shelf. Those wishing to use kitted parts for the turret deletions may use 299 Models' 1/72nd scale conversion kit described in The B-17 Flying Fortress, Part 2. The Hasegawa B-17F and B-17G kits were used for the 1/72nd scale conversions covered below. In 1/48th scale, the same conversions may be done using the Monogram and Revell kits.

YB-40 built from a Hasegawa B-17F in 1/72nd scale. The B-17F kit must be used with a B-17G turret added. The B-17G kit cannot be used because of cheek window problems, and because of the fact that the B-17G kit has a Cheyenne tail turret which is incorrect for the YB-40. Also, the forward top turret needs to be the type used on the B-17F, not the B-17G as used in the Hasegawa kit.

YB-40

The YB-40 can be built using the Hasegawa B-17F as a basis. Up front, the chin turret and fairing from a B-17G kit must be installed, and the cheek windows need to be removed from the B-17F kit. The right waist window must be staggered for the YB-40, but not for the XB-40. Twin guns from the parts box are installed in the waist positions.

On top of the fuselage, the aft portion of the top fairing must be cut back and filled. Then a top turret from a Revell B-26 Marauder kit can be installed in the radio compartment. A mottled olive drab and dark green paint scheme is applied to the upper surfaces, while the undersides are the standard gray.

In 1/48th scale, use a Monogram B-17G with a Monogram B-26 top turret. Stagger the waist windows for the YB-40, and used unstaggered windows on the XB-40. Add the dual guns in the waist positions.

F-9/RB-17G

The B-17G kit from Hasegawa should be used for this conversion in 1/72nd scale. All armament should be deleted, and the remaining holes filled. (Save the parts for use elsewhere! The chin turret and spare guns could be used for the YB-40 conversion explained above.) In place of the chin turret, a trimetrogon chin fairing must be built-up from scratch. Heaters for the nose and radio compartments should be made from scrap plastic.

To make the camera bay, the belly is cut away forward of the ball turret area. Doors should be made from plastic card, and on our model, we installed them in the open position. A sheet plastic spoiler must be installed forward of the camera bay opening.

For our model, the 91st Reconnaissance Squadron insignia was made by hand painting a blue over green diamond, while the knight chasing the devil insignia came from Microscale Sheet 72-72.

In 1/48th scale, the Monogram B-17G could be used and modified with the use of Koster Aero Enterprises Conversion Kit Number 4. Their address is, 223 East Ellis Avenue, Libertyville, Illinois 60048.

Recon F-9/RB-17G of the 91st Reconnaissance Squadron modeled in 1/72nd scale.

QB-17 model of one of the Operation Crossroads aircraft.

QB-17

A Hasegawa B-17G kit can be used to make a QB-17 used in Operation Crossroads. Simply delete all armament, and add the extra antennas as shown on page 43. The outboard wing panels, empannage, and waist should be painted insignia yellow with black bands. We used Scalemaster stripes for the bands on our model. The 58th Bombardment Wing insignia was hand painted, but Microscale is working towards making a decal sheet with these markings.

As with the recon conversion above, the Koster Aero Enterprises kit can be used with a Monogram B-17G to build this QB-17 in 1/48th scale.

MB-17G

Again, the B-17G kit from Hasegawa should be used, and all armament deleted with the resulting holes filled. Use Plastruct rods to build the under-wing launch racks. The JB-2 "Thunderbug" can be built from Scale Model Development Company Kit Number 102. Their address is 7708 Nightingale Drive, Godfrey, Illinois 62035. Some years ago, Heller also made a 1/72nd scale V-1 Buzz Bomb which could also be used.

In 1/48th scale, a Monogram B-17G kit with parts from the Koster Aero Enterprises can be used. The Italeri/Testors V-1 can be used for the JB-2.

GENERAL

The four conversions covered above are the only derivatives included in this book that we actually built. However, any modeler with skills enough to build those four conversions should be able to build almost any derivative covered. We made every effort to include photographs and/or drawings that show all the changes the modeler would have to make. Close-up photographs of the glide bombs should provide sufficient reference material for the modeler to build these from stock kit bombs and plastic stock. We encourage modelers to try the challenge of building these conversions. It is a different and rewarding dimension to the hobby of scale modeling.

The MB-17G makes an interesting model with the JB-2 "Thunderbugs" under the wings.